OUR FOUNDERS
IN THEIR WORDS
AND WHY THEY MATTER

Our Founders in their Words and Why they Matter
Copyright © 2023 by Russell J Rucker

Published in the United States of America
ISBN   Paperback: 979-8-89091-027-1
ISBN   eBook: 979-8-89091-028-8

All rights reserved. No part of this publication may be reproduced, stored in a retrieval system or transmitted in any way by any means, electronic, mechanical, photocopy, recording or otherwise without the prior permission of the author except as provided by USA copyright law.

The opinions expressed by the author are not necessarily those of ReadersMagnet, LLC.

ReadersMagnet, LLC
10620 Treena Street, Suite 230 | San Diego, California, 92131 USA
1.619. 354. 2643 | www.readersmagnet.com

Book design copyright © 2023 by ReadersMagnet, LLC. All rights reserved.

Cover design by Ericka Obando
Interior design by Daniel Lopez

Our Founders in Their Words and Why They Matter

Russell J. Rucker

ReadersMagnet, LLC

TABLE OF CONTENTS

Foreword 9
Chapter 1   The Holidays 15
Chapter 2   Minor Heroes 31
Chapter 3   Hamilton and Jefferson 38
Chapter 4   Thomas Paine 46
Chapter 5   Benjamin Franklin Revolutionary 50
Chapter 6   The Federalist and Anti-
            Federalist Papers 59
Chapter 7   the martyred Nathan Hale 67
Chapter 8   Samuel Adams Father of the
            Revolution 70
Chapter 9   John Hancock First Signor 75
Chapter 10 George Washington Father
            of our Country 79
Chapter 11 James Wilson Associate
            Justice Lawyer 84
Chapter 12 Elbridge Gerry Gerrymandering 88
Chapter 13 John Adams Second President
            of the U.S.A 94

Chapter 14	Alien and Sedition Acts States Response	111
Chapter 15	Richard Dobbs Spaight Duelist	116
Chapter 16	Benjamin Rush Forgotten Father	120
Chapter 17	John Dickinson Penman of the Revolution	124
Chapter 18	Pierce Butler Life in Contradiction	130
Chapter 19	Gouverneur Morris Penman of the Constitution	136
Chapter 20	Robert Morris Financier of the Revolution	140
Chapter 21	In Convention Assembled The Various Plans	144
Chapter 22	Declaration of Independence	162
Chapter 23	The Bill of Rights	170
Chapter 24	Our Constitution as Explained by the Author	179

FOREWORD

From my years of sitting on the bench, I have noticed a lack of understanding, not just of law, but especially of our constitutional rights. Usually, it comes up through challenges do to the Fourth through the Eighth Amendments but not always. I generally do not cite precedents believing that the document itself is where to go.

I am not a historical scholar. I am more of a student of history and in order to understand our Constitution, we have to know why things were done the way they were. This requires knowing the causes and effects of the revolutionary period, in order to understand the circumstances involved in the arguments, which brought certain decisions inside the convention hall. We also need to know where we are today. We need to understand where we've come from and in some cases the reasons. This book was meant to surround what were the events engaging not just our founding, but the reasons and the documents that surround our Constitution.

Some of these causes start with the navigation acts, which forced all ships that did trade with the colonies to be made by England and manned by a majority of British sailors. Over time, the laws were tightened up, which required the numbers to be at least 75% British sailors. This was a way of restricting trade to be between Great Britain and her colonies. In doing so, limiting the trade between the French West Indies. In the process of trying to get revenue from the colonies to pay for the French and Indian war, Britain passed the Sugar Act, the Molasses Act, the Stamp Act, then the Townshend Acts. The colonies fought back by protesting and smuggling in goods.

Britain had war-ships and tried to intervene by chasing down smugglers. During one such chase, smugglers tricked the British vessel Gaspee to chase them across a sandy low point, and the Gaspee was then stuck in the sand, forcing them to wait for high tide to free it. Drums sounded in the providence, and volunteers boarding eight boats went into the sound, surrounding the Gaspee taking it over and burning it. Obviously, Britain was outraged and tried unsuccessfully to get the names of those involved and finally dropped the issue.

Instead of the issues going away, they just kept coming, eventually culminating in war with the colonies, some examples include the seizing of the ship, Liberty, putting the owners on trial, the Boston Massacre, and Boston Tea Party, to name a few. Instead of making the colonies bend to British rule, it did the opposite, it united them against King George III.

It has been my goal, and I have taken it upon myself, to engage people with a better understanding of our rights, through the prism of not just textualism, as defined as the reading of the text, but also an originalist understanding at the time of passage. In order to do this, I have invested in partaking in a historical nature of understanding.

I sincerely hope this, along with my earlier book, will help you to better understand not just the proceedings, but the country itself, so here I give this to you. -The Author.

As we move through the founders and their lives, it paints a real picture of them, their times, and puts together a clearer picture of why things happened the way that they did. To this end, you can understand there really was no other choice in the matter.

With that in mind, I'll start with a personal bugaboo of mine, and that is a lack of respect for our first holidays. The holidays I'm speaking of are those which have their roots in our founding. I just ask you to think about what I'm saying— not necessarily to agree with it all.

Chapter 1
The Holidays

"In Congress July 4th, 1776". Let me start by stating the obvious, July 4th is not the 5th, 8th or 24th of June, August 12th, or any other. As we gather to celebrate July 4th, it's important to understand what we're celebrating, our nation's birth and our independence from Great Britain. I make it a point not to watch fireworks displays on any other date. We fought a great war for independence that lasted a long time. There were pro patriot papers and a dumping of tea in the harbor, with people dressed up as Indians, I might add, protesting the Stamp Act among others. The advantage we had was being on our own soil. Our founders put their lives at risk, and yet there were many who helped in many ways. Warfare in Europe had become too civilized. Two lines lining up in open fields and shooting point blank at each other. The Indians taught us how to fight: hiding behind trees, rocks, a lot of hit and run tactics were used. In the end, we were free independent States able to govern ourselves.

Many point to our founding as suspect, referring to our forefathers as thieves of sacred Indian lands, they refer to the American Indians in the light of some kind of romantic purity. The declaration referred to them as savages in one of their many un-enumerated complaints at the time. In all honesty, that is what they thought of them. A reading of the papers of the day will be enough to show you that.

I have nothing against the Indians. I personally respect them, but they belong to their own nations. Read any number of treaties we signed with them that should be followed, if we still want peace with them, that is. There would have been no need for a treaty, had they not been thought of as nations. But what the Indians aren't, are the original Americans, that honor falls to our founders when they formed this great American nation. The Indians belonged to the

Iroquois, Mohawk, Delawares, and Cherokee Nations. Our founders, as I said, were the original Americans!

Also, regarding slavery often described as America's original sin, it is not America's original sin. In fact, it's not even our sin. It was thrust on us by England, who dumped prisoners on us, sold as indentured servants, and began the slave trade to the colonies. If you care to question it, I give you John Locke's own words from 1690, "Slavery is so vile and miserable an estate of man, and so directly opposite to the generous temper and courage of our nation; (his nation being England) that tis' hardly to be conceived, that an Englishman, much less a gentleman, should plead for it." So, if you so hate the country and don't want to celebrate its birth, that shows it's more of your problem than ours, but I'll raise a glass to you anyway, in the knowledge, that we're all Americans, north and south, east and west. We fought a war that ended slavery, whether you choose to believe that war was over slavery or not. Congress has made both sides, regardless of who they fought for as American veterans. I am in no way defending slavery, and in fact, to the contrary, I've seen the slave quarters where they worked and toiled and honestly, it makes me sick to my stomach, but that doesn't take away from the great things our founders accomplished.

We were a kind of bastard child of England's. I remember it said that the sun never sets on the British Empire. In 1776, we got tired of it and declared independence, fighting off the king's demands. Complaints are listed in the declaration, what we believed was tyranny that the king had forced upon us.

Our founders live on through their words. "We hold these truths to be self-evident, that all men are created equal, that they are endowed by their creator with certain unalienable rights, that among these are life, liberty and the pursuit of happiness," changed from its original draft stating pursuit of property. Many of our citizens, in their confusion, mistake the language of the declaration with that of our Constitution, believing some language is in the other.

They wrote, "That to secure these rights, Governments are instituted among men." It goes on to list complaints to King George and moves on to explain, "that these united colonies are, and of right ought to be free and independent States… we mutually pledge to each other our lives, our fortunes and our sacred honor." The signors were definitely in danger of imprisonment and summary execution by the British, "the Red Coats."

When I was a boy, we celebrated with private fireworks at home more than now. Eventually, the government, in their infinite wisdom, made firecrackers and all exploding fireworks illegal. I understand the injuries from them and the fear of danger, but so goes the price of personal freedom. Now we have large government displays in parks all around, I think we've lost something in the process. The 4th of July is more than picnics, barbeques, and parades. It is the birth of our nation. We should reflect on it; it really was a big deal. We were thousands of miles from Europe, divided by a great sea. We had Indian wars on one side, and were left to fend for ourselves subject to resupply, for what we couldn't produce ourselves. It really should be honored as such. When I watch the fireworks, I think of Francis Scott Key's line, "and the bombs bursting in air, gave proof through the night that the flag was still there". He wrote it after witnessing the all-night barrage of Fort McHenry from a ship in the harbor "Minden", a truce ship, where he was kept under guard, while trying to broker a prisoner exchange during the second war for

Independence in 1814, a war in which they burned our White House.

As Woodrow Wilson cited at Independence Hall during his 4th of July speech, "The declaration of Independence was a document preliminary to war. It was a vital piece of practical business, not a piece of rhetoric." It explains the reasons we must be free from British rule. Those signors knew there would be war, and, in all practicality, they already were at war, as I described earlier. With all respect to Wilson, it is also a document of rhetoric and a call to arms. The same as Paul Revere's ride, one if by land, two if by sea, shining a bright light, there is no greater story of the call to arms than that.

The 4th of July and Washington's birthday were major holidays in the early years of our Republic. As are described in John Spencer Bassett's book, "The Federalist System", from 1906. The colonists celebrated with great balls and parties, their liberty! The fourth of July was often celebrated by the reading of the Declaration of Independence. At least in the first hundred years of our Republic, political debates and speeches were a source of entertainment at one time.

As I raise the flag on the 4th, I'm reminded of those radicals that brought us Independence and honor them. We've moved a long way away from our founding and from our freedoms and liberties that were promised us. I would like to see a return to a better day. Thomas Jefferson was so proud that he listed the Declaration of Independence on his grave as a life accomplishment, being president of the United States is not mentioned. At the end of his life in private letters, he's keeping track of the other signors, remarking with each loss, the few still left. America remains the world's greatest hope for enduring freedom, even as far as we've strayed from her.

So, go on, enjoy the barbeque of brat's, hot dogs', burgers, and steaks, head out to watch the parade, and at dark, make your way to the fireworks- celebrate our nation's birth with the full knowledge of the gift that our founders gave us. The freedom to govern ourselves, it is no small thing, and our greatest gift of all!

So, let's talk about Presidents' Day, or should I say Washington's birthday. I mean, come on! Are Presidents Polk, Hayes, and Tyler as important as Washington and Lincoln? I think not! In the beginning of the Republic, the Federalists celebrated Washington's birthdays with lavish balls and parties. They were celebrating the founding of our country and liberty from England. Jefferson's Republican party refused to celebrate till after his death. The only holiday in the States greater than it was July 4th itself. To see it relegated to such a minor holiday is insulting.

Washington wanted nothing more than to work his plantation. He had the country thrust upon him, first having to fight a war leading our troops and then the Presidency. No one gave more, the list of accomplishments are many, after all, he set up this country, more than anyone else, and yet, was humbled by it all. In the Convention Hall itself, he would open the session and then step aside and listen to all the delegates the States had sent, effectively removing himself from the discussions, or at least making himself less a factor, if that was even possible.

Once Washington was president, he watched his cabinet be torn apart by partisan politics, having both parties fighting for his ear on key issues until Jefferson resigned. Washington warned us about the party system in his farewell address. His farewell address should be required reading. He warns us against entangling alliances with other nations. He gives the best explanation, I've ever heard for taxation, "It is essential that you should practically bear in mind that toward the payment of debts there must be revenue: that to have revenue there must be taxes; that no taxes can be devised which are not more or less inconvenient and unpleasant;" and on parties generally, "they serve to organize faction; to give it an artificial and extraordinary force; to put in the place of the delegated will of the nation the will of the party." and then later goes on, "in the course of time and things to become potent engines by which cunning, ambitious, and unprincipled men will be enabled to subvert the power of the people, and to usurp for themselves the reins of government."

Political parties can be a dangerous thing. President Washington left us after two terms, going back to his plantation and retirement from Government. Washington's birthday is no longer celebrated, or at least relegated to a day off for government workers after watering it down to President's Day. But why does it matter? It matters, because we have relegated our heroes down to nothing in a muse to destroy the Republic in order to set up some other order thereby denying us a republican form of government and the hard-fought liberty... and this from Jefferson's first inaugural address, "We have called by different names brethren of the same principal. We are all Republicans, we are all Federalists. If there be any among us who would wish to dissolve this union or to change its republican form, let them stand undisturbed as monuments of the safety with which error of opinion may be tolerated." Yet this unifying message fell on deaf ears.

So, let's move on to the last great American holiday from our founding, Thanksgiving, turkey day, or whatever other colorful phrase you want to describe it as. We tend to talk about the first Thanksgiving as a harvest celebration with the American Indians in attendance. In which, we are thanking God Almighty for the harvest, but also for religious liberty, which is why the pilgrims were here in the first place.

Of course, still some tell some demented story of a slaughter of Indians at the next Thanksgiving, but as far as our country is concerned, the first National Day of Thanksgiving was proclaimed by our first president. As Washington proclaimed it a National Thanksgiving, in it he begins, "Whereas it is the duty of all nations to acknowledge the providence of Almighty God, to obey his will, to be grateful for his benefits, and humbly to implore his protection and favor." It goes on thanking God for our many blessings, spelling them out basically to thank the Lord for good government in our liberty. "To recommend to the people of The United States a day of public thanksgiving and prayer," both these passages from 1789, which is the first declaration of a public thanksgiving. Then again, in 1795, he proclaims the next Thanksgiving, "I, George Washington, president of the United States, do recommend to all religious societies and denominations, and to all persons whomsoever, within the United States to set apart and observe Thursday, the 19th of February next, as a day of public Thanksgiving and prayer, and on that day to meet together and render their sincere and hearty thanks to the Great Ruler of Nations for..." I point this out to make you understand it wasn't always on a Thursday in November, but it is a thanksgiving to God. This was wholly, a religious nation, despite what our fellow citizens today want us to believe. It was also a religious holiday of sorts.

Then I give you our second President John Adams' rendition from 1798, "As the safety and prosperity of nations ultimately and essentially depend on the protection and the blessing of Almighty God... I have therefore thought fit to recommend, and I do hereby recommend that Wednesday, the 9th day of May next, be observed throughout the United States as a day of solemn humiliation, fasting, and prayer; that the citizens of these States, abstaining on that day from their customary worldly occupations..." What's interesting about John Adams is he's calling for fasting, which would be quite a difference from the pilgrim's feast. Then again in 1799, "As no truth is more clearly taught in the volume of Inspiration, nor any more fully demonstrated by the experience of all ages, than that a deep sense and a due acknowledgment of the governing providence of a Supreme being and of the accountableness of men to him...For these reasons I have thought proper to recommend, and I do hereby recommend accordingly, that Thursday, the 25th day of April, next, be observed throughout the United States of America as a day of solemn humiliation, fasting, and prayer."

It wasn't until 1812 that we have the next proclamation, and this one from a country at war, where Washington's proclamation goes on for pages. Madison's is much shorter and honestly much more interesting, which is why I enclose it in its entirety. Also, the first authorized by a joint session of Congress. All of Madison's proclamations for Thanksgiving are authorized by a joint session of Congress.

"Whereas the Congress of the United States, by a joint resolution of the two Houses, have signified a request that a day may be recommended to be observed by the people of the United States with religious solemnity as a day of public humiliation and prayer: and Whereas such a recommendation will enable the several religious denominations and societies so disposed to offer at one and the same time their common vows and adorations to Almighty God on the solemn occasion produced by the war in which he had been pleased to permit the injustice of a foreign power to involve these United States:

I do therefore recommend the third Thursday in August next as a convenient day to be set a-part for the devout purposes of rendering the Sovereign of the Universe and the Benefactor of Mankind the public homage due to his holy attributes; of acknowledging the transgression which might justly provoke the manifestations of his divine displeasure; of seeking His merciful forgiveness and his assistance in the great duties of repentance and amendment, and especially of offering fervent supplications that in the present season of calamity and war He would take the American people under His peculiar care and protection; that He would guide their public councils, and animate their patriotism, and bestow His blessing on their arms; that He would inspire all nations with a love of justice and of concord and with a reverence for the unerring precept of our holy religion to do to others as they would require that other should do to them; and finally, that, turning the hearts of our enemies from the violence and injustice which sway their councils against us, he would hasten a restoration of the blessings of peace.

Given at Washington, the 9th day of July, A.D. 1812 by the President: James Madison"

Interesting how he asks for prayers for arms, for their enemies to change minds, for forgiveness, and a resumption of peace during this second war for independence.

In 1813, it's the 23rd of July and then in 1814, on November 16th. Madison's final proclamation for the 4th day of March 1815, celebrating an end to war.

"He reared them into the strength and endowed them with the resources which has enabled them to assert their national rights and to enhance their national character in another arduous conflict, which is now so happily terminated by a peace and reconciliation with those who have been our enemies. And to the same divine Author of Every Good and Perfect Gift we are indebted to all those privileges and advantages, religious as well civil..."

Many presidents went on with their proclamations, but these were the only ones from our founders. There were those who just weren't as religious and pious, such as Jefferson and Monroe, who never issued a thanksgiving. These proclamations went on and on until 1942 when President Franklin Roosevelt signed it into law, making it a permanent holiday.

By the late mid-20th century, watching football on Thanksgiving became part of the holiday. So just go ahead, grab a turkey leg, cranberry sauce, and pumpkin pie, watch the games, and enjoy your guests. Lest not forget the reasons are to thank Almighty God for all we have, and that includes our national liberty, as Americans, it's the greatest gift of all!!

All proclamation language came from the 20-volume set *Messages and Papers of the Presidents.* John Locke's words from his book *Two Treaties of Government* published 1690

Chapter 2
Minor Heroes

Many gave their all. Some gave much, and yet some gave little, but still significant accomplishment to the cause of liberty. "The Loyal Nine" and "sons of liberty" come to mind.

It was 1765. The weather was rather harsh and cold in England for several years, but here in the colonies, it was quite mild. King George III had come to the throne, a young man, taken a wife and had a large growing family. Britain had conducted a seven-year war with France and Spain and was carrying a heavy debt. Their reign spanned the globe so much, so, it was said the sun never sets on the British empire. King George III was trying to raise the money through several ventures. One of which was the "British

East India Tea Company", which in reality, was the King himself. What really set off the colonists was the Stamp Act. Instituted by the crown in March 1765, basically imposing a one cent stamp on all paper products cards, books, newspapers, and dice, among other items.

There were roaming mobs in protest around Boston. A shoemaker by the name of Ebenezer Mackintosh was their leader. He could get several thousand in the streets in short order.

There was much hostility after soldiers were quartered among them, and in March 1770, residents threw snowballs and stones at the soldiers, who then responded by firing into the crowd, killing and wounding several of them. A snowball fight basically gone awry. This is what was known as the Boston Massacre.

A group formed, calling themselves the Loyal Nine, their members Henry Bass and George Trott, jewelers; Thomas Chase and John Avery, distillers; and Benjamin Edes, printer of the Boston Gazette along with Steven Cleverly and John Smith both Blazers; Thomas Crafts, a painter; and a ship captain, Joseph

Field. Samuel Adams often met with them but was never a member of the group.

They were focused on repealing the Stamp Act. They hung Oliver, the stamp officer, in effigy and trashed the windows of his home. Not only that, but they burned records and sacked officials' offices. They went on wrecking Governor Hutchinson's fine home, destroying paintings, historical documents, and books by throwing them into the street and setting it all on fire. They passed out anti-Stamp Act literature and had a goal of seeking resignations of those officials. They were very influential and had many magistrates and business owners in fear of them. Twice, the British fled to an island in the harbor for refuge. Also, they went after merchants selling British goods, and finally helped plan the Boston Tea Party. During the tea party protest, they painted themselves, disguised as Indians, who threw tea in the Boston harbor overboard, which was owned by "the British India Tea Company". The goal was to not allow them to earn the tax money. By 1775, the British had responded with troops to suppress the riots. They blockaded the Boston harbor, putting them under siege, demanding payment for the spoiled tea. The other colonies sent goods as supplies ran very low. All trade had stopped. After things got violent, the Loyal Nine tried to distance themselves from the mobs. They eventually all joined the "Sons of Liberty", who carried on their work spying on the British and trying to police themselves as unscrupulous people used their name.

They devised a system to warn the colonists of British troop movements, the Red Coats controlled Boston, but not the surrounding countryside. They organized minutemen for defense, men that could be ready quickly. The British had plans to arrest John Hancock and Samuel Adams and to seize ammunition stores, but much had been dispersed by then. William Dawes and Paul Revere were given the task to ride through the night to warn that the British were coming, talking with militia leaders along the way, warning them, eventually placing lanterns in the north church steeple as a signal, one if by land, two if by sea. Thousands responded to defend against the British troops.

The battle that ensued became our first victory, and the King's representative was sent back to England in shame. We got a much harsher one in his place, but we won the right to fight for our independence.

It was this that was known as the shot heard around the world.

Much has happened in our nation's capital at the state house known as Independence Hall, and yes, I'm speaking of Philadelphia as our nation's capital, which is what it was in those days.

Betsy Ross lived in a small two-story rented house in Philadelphia, that was attached to the rear of a store front, which housed their upholstery shop, with its wood plank floors, a fireplace at one end, and certainly her spinning wheel and looms there. She and her husband ran the upholstery shop. In those days, an upholster sewed about everything, including chairs, drapes, mattresses, pretty much anything you wanted done. George Washington, whom she knew well, a relative of her husband, her uncle, and a signor of the Declaration, George Ross Jr. and Robert Morris, the financier of the Revolution, arrived at her shop to discuss and ask her to sew a flag for the Republic from a rough drawing Mr. Washington had.

The drawing had alternating red and white stripes to represent the individual colonies, with thirteen, white six-point stars representing the united colonies in a new constellation field of blue. Her and her team sewed the first flag using the very drawing Mr. Washington had, suggesting changing the stars on the flag drawing from a six-point star flag to a five-point star flag to increase the efficiency of the work. At the time, these men, less Washington, were all part of a secret committee, the committee of trade, working to finance the war.

According to official records, she received money for sewing flags for warships, and it's important to note, Mr. Morris built and gave warships to the war effort. John and Betsy Ross worshipped at Christ Church in Philadelphia, as did Washington when he was in town, so they certainly knew each other. John Ross, her first husband, and other founders, including Benjamin Franklin, are buried in the churchyard. She is interned with her last husband.

This story shows one more thing. The fact that the colonists were all working together from the wealthiest to the most common. A seamstress would not have been wealthy. Yet, she would have given tremendously for the cause. Her husband, John Ross, as a member of the militia, died in an explosion guarding black powder and munitions. She also had to be cautious, being as she had soldiers quartered in her home.

Let's talk about Betsy Ross for a moment, and the story first publicly told in 1870 by her grandson. I know this is very controversial today due to questions of its accuracy. It has never been proven wrong either! I wonder if it was Washington there that day, or maybe he was with members of this committee. Robert Morris headed the committee and Benjamin Franklin was also a member, too, of the secret committee of trade.

I've always been skeptical of oral history. However, everything in this story seems to fit and should be taken with some credibility. First off, all are placed in the city. It would make sense that her relative, George Ross, would have known Washington and the others, and why not give business to a respected upholsterer who was related to him? It's also true that she was dedicated to the patriot cause. Her second husband died, also in the war effort. He was captured and held. He died while in British custody.

CHAPTER 3
HAMILTON AND JEFFERSON

During Washington's administration, there was a lot of infighting between Hamilton, a British West Indies bastard-born child, an attorney from New York; and Jefferson, a planter, who described himself as hailing from Virginia, a slaveholder, owner of Monticello. Much of the dispute centered around the size of government. Hamilton wanted to build a national road and create a national bank, where the government could keep their funds. He also had a plan to pay off the national debt by paying off three percent per year. Alexander Hamilton was the nation's first Secretary of the Treasury. He is responsible for putting our country's finances on solid footing.

Jefferson's followers believed in a much smaller footprint, but over time, created a much larger government than the Federalists wanted. Jefferson was so in opposition of Hamilton's plans, that he resigned from Washington's cabinet as Secretary of State and formed the Republican party, eventually becoming our third president. This dispute, more than anything else, is why we have a two-party system, and another example of why our founders still matter. Jefferson plotted with Madison to try to expel Hamilton, even after promising Washington that he would attempt to mend fences.

Jefferson used William Giles, a Virginia congressman, to level baseless attacks on Hamilton. Numerous resolutions were sent up accusing Hamilton of maladministration in duties of office, among other things. However, Hamilton was exonerated as all charges were dismissed. When Washington came forward and said two terms were enough, this may very well be the reason.

Hamilton even complained to Rufus King, one of our founders. King would eventually become the last elected Federalist in the country, serving into the mid- 1820's. He confided to Mr. King that he thought it never would end, and Jefferson continued trying to dig up dirt on his political rival. Jefferson was on a personal vendetta of sorts, believing Hamilton and really the rest of the Federalists, of men wanting an aristocracy and guilty of treason.

Jefferson's vice-president, Aaron Burr, killed Hamilton in a duel, and he was tried for murder, though not convicted. Certainly, they drove him to the point where Hamilton thought it necessary.

Hamilton had an affair and was being blackmailed. When Congress found out about the payments, they were concerned, and three congressmen approached him, and he showed them proof through letters that had gone back and forth. This seemed to satisfy them. One of the congressmen was the future President James Monroe. After a few years, it had gone public somehow. It leaked out, and he blamed Monroe, almost causing a duel. When you're engaged in a duel, you have seconds. One of their duties is to try and avert the duel altogether. Aaron Burr had interceded for them, and it was averted, which seems kind of strange after knowing what was to happen.

During the election of 1800, the Electoral College was tied, so it went into the House of Representatives to be settled. The election had been won by the Republicans, but the question was, who would be president, and who would be vice president, Thomas Jefferson, or Aaron Burr? The house was deadlocked. Dozens of votes went by before Hamilton convinced some of the Federalists to support Jefferson. Burr was incensed, especially after Jefferson completely ignored him for his term as vice-president. In 1804, knowing Jefferson would not pick him as his running mate, Burr decided to run for Governor of New York, and after he lost, he was in outrage with Hamilton, because he had written disparaging things against him, and after a few letters were exchanged, he demanded an apology, and he challenged him to a duel.

On the banks of New Jersey, across the Hudson from Manhattan, lies an area in Weehawken, known for being a dueling ground below the cliffs of the palisades in a long-wooded area. There were eighteen known duels held there, including one where Hamilton's son had died three years earlier, but on this summer morning of July 11, 1804, with the deep fog still hanging low, both parties crossed the Hudson River. Rowing from different locations, Burr arrived first, about 6:30 in the morning, and Hamilton just before seven. Dueling was illegal in both New York and New Jersey, so each team tried to give themselves plausible deniability.

The pistols were borrowed from a family friend, the same set his son had used just three years earlier. They were put into a bag, looking much like a small duffel bag today, so each could say they never saw them brought there. Their seconds for the day were facing away from each other, so both could say they never saw shots fired. I think this more than anything else leads to the different stories of the incident. Nathaniel Pendleton and William P. Van Ness both were judges and their seconds, and Hamilton brought Dr. David Hasack. Because Hamilton was challenged, he got to choose which end he was firing from.

Hamilton had both written a letter and told his second he would throw away his first shot. It was considered the gentlemanly thing to do and the reason that in most duels that no one died. But Burr had been practicing, and his intent, as he said later, if it weren't for the sun, he would have shot Hamilton in the heart. This set of dueling pistols held two shots and had a hair trigger as well. The shots were heard almost simultaneously. Hamilton had fired high by fifteen feet and five inches to Burr's left, the bullet went through a cedar branch and lodged in a tree trunk. Burr's shot hit Hamilton's abdomen and ricocheted, hitting other organs as well, and he fell immediately. He rested in Pendleton's arms and said to the doctor, "This is a fatal wound doctor," and then collapsed. They carried him back to the boat and applied smelling salts on the way across, and he became conscious for a moment, warning the others that his pistol was still cocked and loaded and could go off. He died from his wounds later the next day. Burr had warrants out for murder from both States, and he fled into hiding. He was however tried and found not guilty of murder.

Aaron Burr is famous for his conspiracy named after him. Jefferson warned in his annual address, "a great number of private individuals were combining together, arming and organizing themselves contrary to law, to carry on a military expedition against the territories of Spain." The problem was, they couldn't quite figure out whether he was trying to take over Mexico, or a large area of U.S. territory for his own country.

It is my belief that Jefferson did two really great things for us. One, he penned the Declaration of

Independence, setting us on a course in which we would, if not live free, certainly at least be separated from England. The other is the Louisiana purchase, along with the Lewis and Clark expedition. He was mocked for such a large purchase at the time. It nearly doubled the size of our country.

One of the greatest pieces of complaint against Jefferson I ever heard, published in 1802 reads, "a letter to the President of the United States Sir-," and complaining about his inaugural address it goes, "yet after a few sentences you tell us that 'every difference of opinion is not a difference of principle that we are all Republicans—all Federalists… it follows from these declarations, that, in your opinion, the parties have contended not for principles; but for unimportant opinions." I am sure that this over eighty page complaint letter contained within, comes from this extreme vendetta played against Hamilton. The war within our two-party system has never really ended, setting aside the period referred to as the era of good feelings in which the Federalist's had become so weak, they slowly didn't exist anymore. This primarily, following the Alien and Sedition Acts, which were acts of Congress to limit immigration. So, until the

Whig party was organized, they really had no real opposition.

Quotes taken from *Miscellaneous Papers, on Political and Commercial Subjects* by Noah Webster 1802, as well as from *The Compilation of the Messages and Papers of the Presidents.*

Chapter 4
Thomas Paine

Thomas Paine, born in England, some might say, under a bad sign. He had failed marriages and was unhappy with the employment he procured. He met Benjamin Franklin there, who told him to try America, and he went there. Franklin spent a lot of time in England, and then in France as our ambassador, basically living there, returning for brief periods, and then to die in his homeland.

He, Paine, is remembered mostly as a pamphleteer. He wrote and published numerous pamphlets. His "Rights of Man", a defense of the French Revolution, seems strange today, but at the time, public opinion in the States was split on it. The thing about the French Revolution, is that it had an insatiable appetite for mob violence, using the guillotine to chop heads off, then marching them around on sticks, while the mob screams in approval. This is what normally happens in any revolution, whether you want to talk about Mao's China or Hitler's Germany, wherever, millions are murdered. You can never satisfy the mob; this is what makes America so special. It never happened here. There has always been a peaceful transfer of power, that's what makes our founders matter still!

Washington won us independence and then turned in his commission and went home. He never went after those that supported Great Britain.

Paine was a radical, for sure, and had some of his work banned in England and was tried in abstention after he fled to France. Let us not forget all of our founders were radicals of their day.

His most important work, "Common Sense", galvanized the colonies when it came out in 1776 in January, and helped turn the tide of public opinion towards independence. In it, he argues the importance of self-government, describes being the first in any land, having to carve out an existence in the forest to survive, and the importance of working together to have self-government. He states that, "Society in any state is a blessing, but government even in its best state is a necessary evil; … let us suppose a small number of persons settled in some sequestered part of the earth, unconnected with the rest, they will then represent the first peopling of any country, or of the world. In this state of natural liberty, society will be the first thought." He works hard through sixty pages, threading the needle. He argues about the failures of the monarchy: choosing a king and allowing the king to rule for generations. How it foments war and other abuses. "First-That the king is not be trusted without being looked after," and goes on to say, "There is something exceedingly ridiculous in the composition of monarchy; it first excludes a man from the means of information, yet imposes him to act in cases where the highest judgment is required." He even evokes religious examples and states that, "one of the strongest natural proofs of the folly of hereditary right in Kings, is that nature disapproves it, otherwise she would not so frequently turn it into ridicule, by giving mankind an ass for a lion." He weaves about pointing out the number of ships required to protect such a large empire and that we have the makings and ability to build our own navy. He makes it hard, arguing for liberty, to disagree with him. He even brings up the size of the small island governing us, and mentions the events of April 19, 1775, discussed in the chapter on the sons of liberty in chapter two of this book.

In retrospect, it was interesting when I first read it. I don't think I really understood it's context, but I sure see its reality now. It's another piece of the puzzle, which led the public to cry out for independence and work towards the declaration later that year. He was given land in New York for his efforts and buried there, but was not very popular. His bones were dug up and later lost, with the idea of re-burying him with honors in England.

Language taken from *Common Sense* by Thomas Paine 1776.

Chapter 5
Benjamin Franklin Revolutionary

Our revolution occurred during the age of enlightenment. A period in which, there was much advanced thinking and experimentation leading us away from faith-based systems. There was a lot of scientific experiments going on. At parties, people performed parlor tricks, a good example was using static electricity to shock people making their hair stand on end while they all held hands.

Benjamin Franklin was a scientist conducting experiments and was trying to prove that lightning was the same thing, only on a much larger scale, which is why he tied a key onto a kite string during a lightning storm. His experiments on electricity later became the basis for lighting and other later inventions. He invented the lightning rod to save buildings from damage by lightning. This, he gave to the world unpatented. His inventions have changed little since his day. He invented the Franklin stove and chose not to patent it believing it was for the masses. He also invented bifocals, if your over forty, you'll understand their importance.

Testing rainwater in his barrels, he found there was a problem with lead-based paints. It was he that came up with daylight savings time, believing it would save candle wax. His scientific accomplishments gave him international fame. Although it was the printing press that made him wealthy, he had first apprenticed with his father, who was a candlemaker, but he couldn't stand the stench of animal fat. He next apprenticed with his brother, who was a printer. It was here he found his calling. He had access to the books at the printshop and read, studied, and self-educated himself. His brother refused to print his writings, so he wrote under the synonym of Silence Dogood, and they were a big hit. Silence Dogood was a widowed woman. It reads like what it is, a work of fiction. He was good at making things up on the fly. His brother was arrested and served a month or so, refusing to give the names of contributors. The truth is, he didn't know it was his brother. Benjamin had access and kept publishing the paper in his absence. After his brother found out he tried to re-apprentice him, and he ran away to sea lying to a captain saying that he had gotten a girl in trouble and needed to run away.

He spent the next two years in London, surviving by working with printers in various print shops. He had gone there, after a benefactor promised to pay for equipment and set up his own publication. Unfortunately, he reneged on his promise, leaving him to fend for himself.

Two years on, he went to Philadelphia, published a newspaper. He wrote editorials under different pen names to get all sides of the issue, and to fill space, he made up little humorous sayings, and the paper was very well-received indeed. He also published the Poor Richard's Almanack, printed money for the commonwealth and worked on scientific experiments. He set up print shops throughout the colonies, which had to buy paper and ink through him.

Poor Richard's Almanack reads like a serial novel. Each year there is a write up from the fictitious Richard thanking the reader for buying last year's Almanack. "I am excessive poor, and my wife, good woman, is, I tell her, excessive proud; she cannot bear, she says, to sit spinning in her tow, while I do nothing but gaze at the stars; and has threatened more than once to burn all my books and rattling-traps (as she calls my instruments)." There are also what is now famous Franklin quotes. "He that lies down with dogs, shall rise up with fleas," or this, "How many observe Christ's Birth-day! How few, his Precepts! O! 'Tis easier to keep holidays than commandments."

Retiring from printing in his mid-forties, he formed a group of men called the Junto, mostly commoners, they discussed issues and concerns and possible improvements to everyday life. He became immensely successful, and with them, worked for the good of his community, helping to set up a night watch, the city's first police department, a fire department and the nation's first library. They got the streetlights in and lit at night. They founded the first college, which became the University of Pennsylvania.

Later, he was sent to England by the commonwealth of Pennsylvania to sort out the land-holdings of William Penn and stayed there seven years. William Penn had been given a land grant in the previous century and now held three-fourths of Pennsylvania. While there, England passed the Stamp Act in which, all paper cards and even dice sold were taxed a penny and then stamped. England had heavy debt for its wars and was trying to raise money to pay for it. He argued for four hours before their government and managed to get it repealed. He was called in over letters he had written. He came in thinking of himself as an Englishman and left a revolutionary. England thought him a Colonist, and the Colonist thought him an Englishmen. Even with this distrust, he got himself elected to the second Continental Congress and was appointed to a number of committees. He was one of five chosen to write what would become the nation's declaration of independence. Jefferson wrote the first draft, and Franklin suggested changes to the wording of the forward section, "We hold these truths to be self-evident." When it was finished, and

John Hancock signed saying, "we must now all hang together," Franklin finished it by saying, "or we will certainly all hang separately."

That was July 4th, 1776, by October he was sailing to France, his mission, to secure an ally in our war for Independence. Trying to secure France was not easy. He had no leverage, so he played what amounted to a very big poker game, trying to bluff both sides. Finally, following early military victories, France was convinced and war between France and England commenced. The problem was France was sending, secretly, small arms. They were fighting England in areas which were not aiding us. Franklin asked for more, trying to get France to put an army on American soil to help. John Adams was sent to aid Franklin, but he was not well received. His view of diplomacy did not work well. Franklin smoothed the edges, romancing France into help, whereas Adams was blunter, and wound-up undermining efforts he was making. Franklin tried to get Adams recalled, and he was sent to Holland. Benjamin Franklin was an excellent diplomat respecting the royalty, flirting with the ladies, getting them to help with their husbands. Spies were everywhere, and even with them, he was able to use them to his benefit. Regular reports sent back to England alarmed them as well, but in the end, he had shown how to make diplomacy work. Not only had he gotten a deal with France, but also Spain, their ally, followed, too.

When he finally came home, it was to a home his wife had built, but in his absence she had died. He had come home to die in his America. He loved his life in France and England, but America was his home. In those early years, Philadelphia was our capital. We had been living under first, the Continental Congress and then the Articles of Confederation. They just weren't strong enough for our new country.

In the hot summer months of 1789, delegates from all over the new country gathered in Philadelphia to pound out a Constitution. First it was to improve, amend make changes to the Articles of Confederation, but Madison had brought his own plans. He had spent months studying self-government everywhere it had been tried. Pinckney had his own plan as well, and later even New Jersey offered up a plan. Washington would open each day's meetings, and then step aside in an effort to minimize his stature. This should really not surprise anyone, as he had turned in his commission at the end of the war and went home to his beloved Mount Vernon. George Washington could have swayed anyone, and Ben Franklin, by now, was an aging statesman. He also suffered badly from gout and had to be carried in on an invention of his, basically a chair with two long rods. It looked kind of like the Ark of the Covenant. He lived in Philadelphia, so he was there the entire time. Some came late to the point of not having a quorum right away. Some came, then left, not happy with the new direction. The States had sent their most influential men, but it wasn't until August, that the hard work had been completed, and all done in secrecy, they were all working under the confines of a gag order. He made a final plea for the delegates to sign, "In these sentiments, sir, I agree to this Constitution, with all its faults, if they are such," earlier "I confess that there are several parts of this constitution which I do not at present approve, but I'm not sure that I will never approve of them." Citing his ability over time to change course, then began the work of getting the States to agree to it, some went home and fought ratification, others worked for it, which brings us to the Federalist and anti-Federalist papers. On an odd note, he wanted the turkey to be our national bird, good thing it's the bald eagle today.

Franklin was interned at Christ Church in Philadelphia. Twenty thousand people attended. In France, there was a public mourning. For all his trappings, he has been called the first American.

Quotations from *Poor Richards Almanack* published by Benjamin Franklin, various years and *The Records of the Federal Convention of 1787* by Max Farrand.

CHAPTER 6
THE FEDERALIST AND ANTIFEDERALIST PAPERS

The Federalist papers are a series of 85 essays, written by Madison, our fourth president, and father of the Constitution. John Jay, our first Chief Justice of the High Court, and Hamilton, our first Secretary of the Treasury, they got a group of articles published in papers, editorials arguing for ratification of our Constitution by the State of New York. Writing as "Publius", I must confess my desire to go on and on knowing I won't know where to stop. The debate on ratification of the Constitution comes right out of the convention and spills into the streets. In papers, articles are written not just as Publius but as Cato, Brutus, an American citizen, all well-written for sure, arguing back and forth, after all, nothing is more important as one's Constitution.

New York was the eleventh State to ratify. By that time the nine States required had already passed. New York was important due to its size.

"Z" replies to Franklin's speech at the end of the convention, that, he, Franklin, shed a tear, and tries to tear it apart, I think unsuccessfully.

Hamilton writing first as himself stating the "weight of influence of the persons who framed it," and mentions the dissent of two or three important men. He argues for the passage of the document. His way of arguing as "Publius" simply weighs too heavy against those dissenting. Writing as, "An American Citizen", talking about how the Unites States was settled, "want of charity in the religious systems of Europe and of justice in their political governments were the principal moving causes, which drove the emigrants of various countries to the American continent. The Congregationalists, Quakers, Presbyterians and other British dissenters, the Catholics of England and Ireland, the Huguenots of France, the German Lutherans, Calvinists, and Moravians." Keeping in mind, with no Bill of Rights at this time, we were arguing over ratification without them. The founders believed they were within the document itself, therefore unnecessary. He also argues for our state constitutions established after independence.

And "in designating the nature of the chief executive office of the United States, have deprived it of all the dangerous appendages of royalty.... As our President bears no resemblance to a king, so we shall see the Senate have no similitude to nobles," and "will have none of the peculiar follies and vices of those men," and speaking of Congress itself, states quite clearly, I think, "They can hold no other office, civil or military under the United States, nor can they join in making provisions for themselves." He argues that the judges may not be so free from presidential and Senate pressures due to their appointments. His third article complains about the size of Congress, claiming it could be too numerous, even talks about the importance of maturity of the congressman, and sums up, "such the foundations of peace, liberty and safety, which have been laid by their unwearied labors – they have guarded you against all servants by those 'Whom choice and common good ordain,' against all masters 'Save preserving Heaven.'"

"Cato" argues that, and I quote as I often do here that, "Government, to an American, is the science of his political safety," and points out the successful campaign for independence against what was the world's most powerful force. In it he instructs you to, "Deliberate, therefore, on the new national government with coolness; analyze it with criticism; and reflect on it with candor," clearly asking you to carefully think it over and examine it. He asks you to look for faults, "if there are any." In other words, to proceed with caution!

By the time we get to his second essay editorial, he is arguing back and forth with someone writing under the pen name of "Caesar", yes, I know this isn't ancient Rome, but what you must keep in mind is the classical education all these people had. They all studied Rome and ancient Greek governments. What comes to my mind is, if I were to write up an editorial today, they would want my name, address, e-mail, and phone number. These men were all writing with pen names. It would not be tolerated today. It would simply not be printed.

"Remember o' my friends! The laws, the rights, The generous plan of power deliver'd down By your renown'd forefathers.

So dearly bought the price of so much blood!

O let it never perish in your hands!

But piously submit it to your children."

He rips apart "Caesar", when he argues you must accept it all without amendments.

"Caesar" tells us to reject it if we have to proceed cautiously. He cites if, "the convention in one word is dissolved", if so, we must, "reject it, in toto, or vice versa just take it as it is; and be thankful."

"Centennial" argues, "Before you surrender these great and valuable privileges up forever. Your present frame of government, secures you to a right to hold yourselves, houses, papers and possessions free from search and seizure, and therefore warrant granted without oaths of affirmations first made, affording sufficient foundations for them." You see, as we go through these objections, what they are really arguing for, is a Bill of Rights to be submitted along with the Constitution. In many cases, you find the exact wording of our present Bill of Rights.

James Wilson, one of the delegates to the convention, speaks, trying to explain many of the points in contention. But, writing under the pseudonym "Democratic Federalist", states a rebuttal, "To those that object, that a Bill of Rights has not been introduced in the proposed Federal Constitution, if this doctrine is true, and since it is the only security that we are to have for our natural rights, it ought at least to have been clearly expressed in the plan of Government," and goes on to explain that, "in the 2nd section of the present Articles of Confederation says; each State retains its sovereignty, freedom and independence." They are clearly concerned that this is something they are giving up potentially. They want some insurance against the natural rights they will forfeit.

"Brutus" writes, "Perhaps this country never saw so critical a period in their political concerns…At length a convention of States has been assembled, they have formed a constitution which will now probably, be submitted to the people to ratify or reject." He asks whether this current type of confederate government is best for us, or whether it should be reduced to one great Republic, or whether we should carry on as individual States. This is really the question of the day. He goes on for pages, explaining the text in detail, but in the end argues to reject it as he cites that, "it creates the whole union into one government, under the form of a Republic.…and if I did not in my conscience believe that this scheme was defective in the fundamental principles- in the foundation upon which a free and equal government must rest -I would hold my peace." So, here we have another of the great concerns, that being, we are establishing too strong a federal government. Much more of a dissent than that of a Bill of Rights. After all, a Bill of Rights could be and would be added through the amendment process.

"A Citizen of Philadelphia" goes long in a rebuttal, basically arguing that we have already seen an advantage to holding as one great country. It is in this environment that Hamilton, Jay and Madison begin their vigorous defense on the proposed Constitution. Writing under the synonym of "Publius". "The subject speaks its own importance; comprehending in its consequences, nothing less than the existence of the UNION, the safety and welfare of the parts of which it is composed, the fate of an empire, in many respects, the most interesting in the world." They argue for the rights of man, against a second convention insisting in its danger. This goes on for their eighty-five essays back and forth with the others in contention, explaining how the system of government will work. Never giving an inch, and in the end, they're the ones that achieved this immense victory!

However, the opposition did get an important victory because in Sept 1789, Congress passed a proposed Bill of Rights and sent them to the States. So, why do the founders still matter? The Bill of Rights passed almost immediately most of them. Two remained for over 200 years, our last amendment passed in 1992. That being one of the original Bill of Rights. Our founders aren't just the signors. They encompass all the patriots of their time. On both sides of the argument.

All quotations come from the two-volume set *Debate on the Constitution* last known published date 1955.

CHAPTER 7
THE MARTYRED NATHAN HALE

Nathan Hale was educated at Yale. Sent there with his older brother at age 14, he graduated at 17 with high honors and took a job as a schoolteacher, which is where he was when the war broke out. He joined the Connecticut militia. Following the battles of Lexington and Concord the unit was called up. Two of his brothers enlisted. He stayed behind, as he had a contract to teach, and he felt duty bound by it. But shortly after receiving a letter back from the conflict, which greatly inspired him as many of our founders, he too was a common man called into action, and after fulfilling his teaching duties, he enlisted and was given the rank of captain. The British had captured New York, and Washington was looking for information on troop movement in an effort to take back the city. General Washington asked for volunteers to spy on the British, and Nathan Hale was the only one who volunteered for the dangerous mission.

He disguised himself as a Dutch schoolmaster looking for work and procured a ferry to cross the river to New York leaving his uniform behind. About the time he arrived, the city was under fire. A quarter of it burned. He had a certificate from Yale and other documentation with him and dressed in a brown coat. He should have been convincing, but got caught due to asking too many questions. He was brought to General Howe, and he didn't deny what he was doing there. He was sentenced to death as an enemy combatant and hanged in a tree. His body was never found. The British reportedly buried him close by.

Gone only a few days before his execution after he was found guilty, he requested a bible, which was denied, and then a parson, which was also denied. The morning of his execution, he was given an opportunity to write letters, of which, he wrote two, one of which was to his mother. The British tore them up in front of him and proceeded with the hanging. His speech before the gallows is why he's remembered. He was very composed with no sorrow or fear, only focused on what was before him, according to those present, and it was reported that he said, "It is the duty of all soldiers to follow the orders of his commander and chief, and that he should be willing to except death for his country in any manner and at any turn and that I regret that I have but one life to lose for my country," or something along those lines. The later part was a popular line used by his college friends from the play, "Cato". It is suggested he used this line as the British soldiers would understand their meaning, as Cato was a very well-known play of the day. At the time, we were losing the war, and his arrest and summary execution left him martyred. His death became a call to arms, so even in death, he aided his patriot comrades. It also helped Washington in understanding the importance and the establishment of a well-trained spy force, as Hale was sent in with little to no training or direction, told only to gather as much information as possible.

Chapter 8
Samuel Adams
Father of the Revolution

Samuel Adams was born in Boston into a politically active and religious family. He went first to their Latin school and then was sent to Harvard. He wanted a career in law, but at his mother's urging, he took a job in the counting house of a local merchant, but was quickly fired. The owner believed him too interested in politics. That really hits the nail on the head it seems. That's all he was interested in.

His father loaned him a thousand pounds. He loaned out half to a friend and squandered the rest and went to work at his father's brewery and malt shop. He even failed at collecting taxes for Boston, a position he had been elected to. Boston sued him for his failure to collect the taxes. He helped establish a local newspaper, the "Independent Advertiser", and even managed to fail at that. Adams really had no business sense at all. His family had hoped he would become a reverend. He had a great gift for oratory and knew how to move a crowd. He married Elizabeth Checkley, a pious daughter of a minister, and set about raising a family.

Britain passed the Sugar Act, in an effort to raise revenue, the act taxed molasses imports from the West Indies, and he fought that, as well as the Stamp Act. Taxes had to be paid in hard currency, which was in very limited supply. His father helped set up a land bank, a scheme in which printed money was lent against property and accepted as payment for goods. Eventually, Britain closed it down, and left the landowners bankrupt, owing great sums, which couldn't be repaid. This left the younger Adams much in distrust of government.

He was instrumental in, and met with, but was not a member of the Loyal Nine, and later on the Sons of Liberty. John Hancock and Samuel Adams were the ones who the British were looking for, which sparked the battles of Concord and Lexington. Samuel Adams was not just a casual observer of the revolution. It didn't come to him. He instigated and fermented not just malt liquor but was also the cause of the revolution in the first place, and on the morning of April 19th, 1775, upon hearing the gunshots at Lexington, he's quoted as saying, "What a glorious Morning for America."

He was elected to the Massachusetts general court. He wrote resolutions defending citizens' rights of liberty. He was elected clerk of the house; he urged shopkeepers not to import goods from England, instituting a boycott. He helped to get the mobs in the street, was instrumental in the planning of riots and rebellion. Writing under pen names, he railed against the British, and helped organize the Boston Tea Party as well. Although there is no evidence that he participated in it, he fanned the flames of rebellion and was a true fighter for liberty. Following the Boston Massacre, a protest snowball fight gone wrong, soldiers were made to stand trial, and Samuel Adams argued that troops should be removed before there was any more bloodshed.

John Adams and Josiah Quincy defended them at trial after the urging of Samuel, and they were found not guilty as they claimed they fired in self-defense. Three had died instantly. Two more died later from their injuries. He used the incident to keep the colonists worked up for independence from Britain.

Adams offered up a resolution, forming a committee on correspondence, and a declaration of rights for colonists. He served in both Continental Congresses, when Richard Henry Lee of Virginia proposed a resolution calling for independence from Britain. He cast his vote for and signed The Declaration of Independence. In his speech, he states, "Our Union is now complete; our Constitution composed, established, and approved. You are now the guardians of your own liberties…The people of this country alone have formally and deliberately chosen a government of themselves, and with open uninfluenced consent bound themselves to a social compact." In his lengthy speech he argues for independence, something he's spent his life fighting for. Due to the secrecy, as Congress was working behind closed doors, there is very little known of his actions following the Declaration. He spent the rest of his career in elected State offices, and his national career came to an end. Upon his death, he was immortalized as the father of the revolution. Surely, if liberty and freedom still matter, so does the legacy of Samuel Adams, which is a free American Republic.

Quotes taken from the *Oxford Dictionary of Political Quotations* edited by Antony Jay. And from the speech *American Independence 8-1-1776.*

CHAPTER 9
JOHN HANCOCK FIRST SIGNOR

"Put your Hancock here," a statement made every day, when signing loan papers or other documents, a reference to the first signor of the Declaration of Independence. John Hancock was born in Braintree, Massachusetts, now Quincy. He was the son of a prominent reverend, but at age seven, his father passed away, and he was sent to live with his aunt and uncle. They were importers and merchants in Boston, and after graduating from Harvard, he went to work for his uncle's business, "The House of Hancock". It was a very successful business, and they were very wealthy. John often rode around town in a fine elaborate gold coach and wearing the finest, most elaborate clothing. He even spent a year in Europe, learning about the trade. Upon his uncle's death, he inherited his uncle's business. His business made him very popular and was, at one time, the wealthiest merchant in the colonies. If he didn't have what you needed or wanted, he could get it for a price, of course. America was primarily an agricultural country, and most goods of want had to be imported, from fine China to tea.

He was elected to office, at a time when Britain was trying to tax the colonies first with the Sugar Tax, which taxed the import of molasses. Then the Stamp Act, and later, the Townshend acts, which taxed lead, paint, paper, ink, porcelain, glass, and tea and allowed the British to go into anyone's home and seize products. In order to get around the taxes and tariffs, the colonists took to smuggling. He helped organize the boycott of British goods, timidly at first. His ship, Liberty, was seized, and he was put on trial for smuggling. In court, he was successfully defended by John and Samuel Adams. He, along with Samuel Adams, led the Sons of Liberty through many violent protests involved in the planning stages, including the Boston Tea Party. His speech following the Boston Massacre is his most famous and was printed and distributed throughout the colonies, "is the present system, which the British administration have adopted for the government of the colonies, a righteous government -or is it tyranny?...And also as a faithful subject of the state, to use his upmost endeavors to detect, and have detected, strenuously to oppose, every traitorous plot which its enemies may devise for its destruction. Security to the persons and properties of the governed is so obviously the design and end of civil government, that to attempt a logical proof of it would be like burning tapers at noonday, to assist the sun in enlightening the world."

When the British marched out of Boston to Lexington and then Concord with a warrant for them both and orders to seize weapon stores, he and Samuel Adams were together in Lexington. Paul Revere, during his famous ride, stopped and warned him and Samuel Adams, then rode on. Upon returning, Revere found John Hancock still there, with no intent on leaving. He thought he could be of some use, defending with the minutemen, but Revere told him he had no musket, and that he'd be a big prize for the British, and more importantly, he was more valuable as a leader and convinced him to leave. Colonists were offered immunity if they go back and live as British subjects. Everyone except Samuel Adams and John Hancock that is! Later, while serving in the Continental Congress, he signed the declaration of independence with his signature being very large. Reportedly, saying it was so the king could read it without his glasses. He also served as Massachusetts first and third governor of our new Republic.

Speech insert was taken from the *Boston Massacre commemoration speech* given in 1774.

CHAPTER 10
GEORGE WASHINGTON
FATHER OF OUR COUNTRY

Washington was a quiet, peaceful man. He did not seek revolution. It just came to him, a very pious man, reading sermons to his wife, quietly praying morning and night. There are stories of bullet holes through his clothing, and yet he was never hit. He even found time to pray on the battlefield.

Content on living on his plantation, he was the wealthiest plantation owner of his day. He exemplified Virginia hospitality and housed visitors, who wandered up the river that far. He began planting tobacco, but switched his main crop to flour, milling it there. His, Mt. Vernon Flour Company was regarded as the best, as well as his horses. He distilled rye whisky.

In autumn, he had invited guests for the hounds and hunt.

Time and time again, his country called him, and he answered that call. After the war for Independence, he said farewell to his troops and turned in his commission and went home. He spent fourteen years away at war. His military service began in 1754, during what would become the French and Indian war and served on and off until 1783.

In the Continental Congress, on July 2nd, 1776, while discussing the Declaration of Independence, he said, "The time is now near at hand which must probably determine whether Americans are to be freemen or slave; whether they are to have any property they can call their own…the fate of unborn millions will now depend, under God, on the courage and conduct of the army. Our cruel and unrelenting enemy leaves us only the choice of brave resistance, or the most abject submission. We have, therefore, to resolve to conquer or die."

At the convention, he would open each day's meeting as the president of the Convention, and then step aside and allowed the chair of the committee of the whole to take over everything. He rarely spoke. He knew of the weakness of the Articles of Confederation and wanted a break from it with a vigorous federal government.

He served years as a member of the house of Burgesses. There, he was known as "The Virginia Patriot". He also served in the Continental Congress. Patrick Henry spoke of him saying, "If you speak of solid information and sound judgment, Colonel Washington is unquestionably the greatest man on that floor." He was even a freemason and served as master of his lodge.

Charles Thomas Esq. was sent to dispatch a message to Washington from Congress, upon his election to the presidency. "I have now, sir, to inform you that the proofs you have given of your patriotism, and of your readiness to sacrifice domestic ease and private enjoyments to preserve the happiness of your country, did not permit the two Houses to harbor a doubt of your undertaking this great and important office, to which you are called not only by the unanimous vote of the electors, but by the voice of America." Washington's response, "I have been accustomed to pay so much respect to the opinion of my fellow citizens that the knowledge of their having given their unanimous suffrages in my favor scarcely leaves me the alternative for an option. I cannot, I believe, give greater evidence of my sensibility of the honor which they have done me than by accepting the appointment." When arriving in New York, the chancellor of New York Robert Livingston swore him in as president of the United States, using a Bible borrowed from a nearby church, before a large crowd and he turned to Congress and gave an opening address to them.

He went on to serve eight years as president of the United States, helping to set up a government that he worked on in the late convention. He is described as a Federalist but is the only president to never belong to any political party. In his farewell address, he railed against and warned us all about them. He was a humble man called on again and again by his countryman. Really, nothing more than that. He gave up the presidency after two terms to go home to his beloved Mt. Vernon. The whole idea of serving a few years and then going home was his way of life. Much has been made of late of his ownership of slaves. His will freed his slaves, upon his wife's death, in it he ordered them taught to read and write, to prepare them to be self-sufficient, and he paid those unfit to work a subsistence for life out of his estate. He had become disgusted by slavery and an abolitionist, trying to find a way to end the practice.

Upon his death, he was eulogized, "First in War, First in Peace, First in the hearts of our countryman."

Information and quotes taken from *Messages and Papers of the Presidents Vol. 1.* Some quotes from *The Oxford Dictionary of Political Quotes.*

Chapter 11
James Wilson
Associate Justice Lawyer

James Wilson went to college in Scotland, but never finished there. He moved to Philadelphia where he studied and was given an honorary degree in Master of Arts, and he taught Latin, English, and Greek at the College of Philadelphia. Then he turned his attention to the law and studied under John Dickinson who was a statesman and delegate to the first Continental Congress and eventual signor of the Declaration of Independence. He opened a law practice and became a wealthy and influential attorney.

He published a pamphlet entitled "Considerations on the Nature and extent of the Legislative Authority of the British Parliament". In it, he argues that parliamentary authority ends at the British shores. This made Wilson's fame spread throughout the colonies and he became a member of the Committee of Correspondence and was elected to the Second Continental Congress. It was this Congress that sent a committee to work on the Declaration of Independence which consisted of Thomas Jefferson, Benjamin Franklin, Robert Sherman, Robert R. Livingston, and John Adams. Wilson became one of the signors and has the distinction of being one of only six of our founding fathers who signed both the Declaration and the Constitution.

He got in trouble defending loyalists in court and was considered a traitor, even though he had signed the Declaration of Independence. A large number of men gathering at Burns Tavern got drunk and went after merchants and eventually tried to storm Wilson's home where a number of men had gathered, in the pursuing fight, the first floor of the house was set on fire, gunfire rang out and, in the end, there were fourteen wounded, and six laid dead. Wilson fled to Robert Morris's estate outside of town, some of the drunken men were arrested and the attackers were eventually pardoned.

During the Constitutional Convention, he served on the committee of detail. which was given the task of writing up what they had agreed on, to set it into a final working document. He argued against the Electoral College and was an active member in the convention hall. Later, he gave a speech in defense of the Constitution which was very influential and printed throughout the colonies. It had more influence than the Federalist papers, due to the fact that Federalist papers being largely published in New York, and his speech being distributed in twelve of the thirteen colonies.

In it, he explains that, and this is the vital point, "Hence it is evident, that in the former case, everything which is not reserved, is given, but in the latter, the reverse of the proposition prevails, and everything which is not given is reserved. This distinction being recognized, will furnish an answer to those who think an omission of a Bill of Rights, a defect in the proposed Constitution," in this speech, he lays naked all the main arguments of those opposed to the document, and in the end, he sums it up in this way, "I will confess indeed, that I am not a blind admirer of this plan of government, and that there are some parts of it, which if my wish had prevailed, would certainly have been altered. But, when I reflect how widely men differ in their opinions, that every man (and the observation applies likewise to every State) has an equal pretension to assist his own, I am satisfied that anything nearer to perfection could not have been accomplished." This speech is used to this day too understand originalist judicial theory.

Wilson was appointed by President Washington as one of the original associate justices of the Supreme Court, where he served until death nine years later. In the Supreme Court case Chisholm vs Georgia, a 4 to 1 decision was arrived. He sides with the majority against the state. Georgia never defended itself believing the federal government had no jurisdiction. This case led to the Eleventh Amendment reversing their decision for future cases anyway. In the end, James Wilson had a seat to determine the meaning of the Constitution he helped write. The Constitution itself is why the founders still matter!

Exact language of his speech taken from *The Debate on the Constitution* published 1955.

CHAPTER 12
ELBRIDGE GERRY GERRYMANDERING

Elbridge Gerry was born in Marblehead Massachusetts in 1744, into a politically active family. His father, among other positions he held, was Justice of the Peace. He was a wealthy merchant shipper and owned his own vessels. Eldridge entered Harvard at age fourteen and earned both a bachelor's and master's degrees. It was not uncommon for boys of that age to be sent to college. After graduation, he went to work in his family's counting house, they shipped dried fish to Spain and Barbados. He was opposed to the Stamp Act and served on a committee, trying to enforce bans on the import of tea.

His father served on the committee of correspondence and soon Eldridge joined him there as well. He was elected to the general court where he met Samuel Adams, and he quickly became enamored with him and in the fight for liberty. During the British blockade of Boston, Marblehead became an important alternate port. Gerry was quick in his procurement of arms and ammunition to be sent to the Boston area.

Gerry had been appointed to the provincial Congress, and later to the executive committee of safety. During Paul Revere's famous ride, he was at the "Menotomy Tavern" where he had attended an important meeting with two American colonels. When a detachment of Red Coats searched the tavern, they fled into the cornfield into hiding while the British passed.

He remained in Boston procuring arms and supplies for the patriots. Gerry proposed a law in Congress to arm and equip vessels for war ships. John Adams had said it was one of the most important laws passed.

He was elected to the second Continental Congress where he encouraged members from the middle colonies to aid in support of independence.

John Adams' citing of Gerry, "If every man here was a Gerry, the liberties of America would be safe against the gates of Hell and earth." He voted for and signed "the Declaration of Independence". He is also a signor of "the Articles of Confederation." Later, he became offended at actions he felt were against personal liberties and walked out over a disagreement over a price schedule for suppliers, although technically a member, he remained absent for years from his seat. Adams, in his criticism of him cited, "He will risk great things to secure small ones." He supported resolutions against fasting, days of prayer and horse racing, among others.

He was elected to the Massachusetts house of representatives and was sent to the Federal Convention as a delegate. Another delegate said, "he opposed everything he did not propose." one of only three to later refuse to sign it. In his final speech on the convention floor, he described the painful feelings of his situation this way, "I hope I should not violate the respect in declaring on this occasion my fears that a civil war may result from the present crises of the U.S.- In Massachusetts, particularly I see the danger of this calamitous event- in that State there are two parties, one devoted to Democracy, the worst I think of all political evils, the other as violent in the opposite extreme." His main complaints were a lack of a Bill of Rights and the vice president as president of the Senate, a position he would later hold. He even opposed the great compromise, which made two branches of the legislature, one branch the Senate with its equal representation, and the other, the House, representing the population. He later fought ratification, his complaints included "inadequate representation of the people, dangerous and ambiguous legislative powers, a blending of the legislature and the executive branches, and the endanger of an oppressive judiciary." An anti-Federalist, to the dismay of his friends, later served in Congress supporting Federalist policies. When arguing in Congress for the Bill of Rights, he stated "What, sir is the use of a militia? It is to prevent the establishment of a standing army, the bane of liberty, whenever government means to invade the rights and liberties of the people, they always attempt to destroy the militia, in order to raise an army upon their ruins."

President John Adams sent Charles Pinckney, John Marshall, and Eldridge Gerry to France to work out a peace treaty with them following the

French Revolution. The French wanted a payment of bribes which they refused. This was known as the XYZ Affair, after signature lines noted on the document. Gerry stayed behind and tried to smooth out affairs which kept us out of war with them. When he returned, he found anger against him as the others had blamed him for the trip's failure. Eventually, the treaty of Mortefontaine was completed keeping us in neutrality in a war between France and England to the credit of the Adams administration.

He ran for Governor of Massachusetts first, unsuccessfully; as a Republican, a later election was successful, and he was governor during the redistricting process. As governor, he signed a law which put legislative maps in place which gave out power to himself and his party, one of the proposed districts was in the shape of a salamander, and he was mocked in the paper as Gerry-mandering. Which is why that term applies to all unfair political maps. He became unpopular for abuses of office like appointing family members to posts and suing papers for libel opposed to his parties' views. Just before being voted out of office, James Madison chose him as his running mate, and he served as Madison's vice-president.

With the war of 1812 becoming very unpopular and Congress increasingly divided, he became important as the president of the Senate a position he had opposed in the Constitutional Convention. He was active in the parties and balls, all the pomp and circumstance of the Washington elite, a favorite of Dolly Madison. In November 1814, he had a heart attack and still tried to take his carriage to the Senate where he served as the president of the Senate but had to be taken back and carried to his bed and he died there, leaving his wife broke sleeping on the streets. The Senate passed a bill giving his salary to his widow, but it died in the house, believing it a bad precedent.

Today, he is most remembered and matters most for his Gerrymandering and political tactics. He remains the only founder buried in D.C. Congress paid for his cemetery monument.

Quotes in convention taken from *The Records of the Federal Convention of 1787* by Max Farrand, some quotes from *A-Z quotes.com*.

CHAPTER 13
JOHN ADAMS SECOND PRESIDENT OF THE U.S.A.

John Adams was born in Braintree Massachusetts, now Quincy, to a modest family his father was a farmer and shoemaker. A well-educated young man, he attended Harvard and took a job teaching in a Latin school to help pay for his studies in law. His parents had hoped it would be in the ministries. But he studied law with a prominent local lawyer.

In 1758 he started his legal career but having a rocky start. His first year in office he had only one client and it took him three years before winning a case. By 1770, he had a highly successful law practice in Boston. He successfully defended the British soldiers following the Boston Massacre. This was important because it showed the British that the colonist could be trusted with fair judicial authority.

He at first was reluctant to join the cause for liberty fearing for his law practice, but eventually, wrote anonymously articles in the local papers under the pressure and convincing from his cousin Samuel Adams. At the time, they were fighting Britain over the taxation the colonists were so opposed too.

He was elected to the first and then the second Continental Congress, where he took an active role in arguing for "the Declaration of Independence". He sat on more than ninety committees in Congress, more than anyone else, including the one responsible for writing "The Declaration of Independence" and if it weren't for him, it most likely would not have passed, most were opposed before he took the floor.

In a letter to his wife, he wrote "I am well aware of the toil and blood and treasure, that it will cost us to maintain this Declaration, and support and defend these States. Yet through all the gloom I can see the rays of ravishing light and glory. I can see that the end is more than worth all the means and that posterity will triumph in that day's transaction even altho we should rue it, which I trust in God, we shall not."

Here, I give you the original draft language of the "Declaration of Independence" before it was changed and modified to appease those who always want to water things down. It is really interesting to read its original intent. Keeping in mind this was Jefferson, Franklin, Sherman, Livingston and Adams original intent and vision. Be it true that it's these same men working on it, that altered it for the inevitable purpose of its passage.

I have chosen to number the complaints for the reader's benefit.

"A Declaration by the representatives of the United States of America, in General Congress Assembled.

When in the course of human events it becomes necessary for one people to dissolve the political bands which have connected them with another, and to assume among the powers of the earth the separate and equal station to which the laws of nature and of nature's god entitle them, a decent respect to the opinions of mankind requires that they should declare the causes which impel them to the separation.

We hold these truths to be self-evident; that all men are created equal; that they are endowed by their creator with inherent and inalienable rights.

That among these are life, liberty and the pursuit of happiness; that to secure these rights, governments are instituted among men, deriving their just powers from the consent of the governed. That whenever any form of government becomes destructive of these ends, it is the right of the people to alter or to abolish it, and to institute new government, laying its foundation on such principles, and organizing its powers in such form, as to them shall seem most likely to affect their safety and happiness. Prudence indeed will dictate that governments long established should not be changed for light and transient causes; and accordingly all experience hath shewn that mankind are more disposed to suffer while evils are sufferable than to right themselves by abolishing the forms to which they are accustomed but when a long train of abuses and usurpations begun at a distinguished period and pursuing invariably the same object, evinces a design to reduce them under absolute despotism it is their right, it is their duty to throw off such government, and to provide new guards for their future security. such has been the patient sufferance of these colonies; and such is now the necessity which constrains them to expunge their former systems of government, the history of the present king of Great Britain is a history of unremitting injuries and usurpations, among which appears no solitary fact to contradict the uniform tenor of the rest but all have in direct object the establishment of an absolute tyranny over these States. To prove this, let facts be submitted to a candid world for the truth of which we pledge a faith yet unsullied by falsehood."

1. "He has refused his assent to laws the most wholesome and necessary for the public good."

2. "He has forbidden his governors to pass laws of immediate and pressing importance, unless suspended in their operation till his assent should be obtained; and when so suspended, he has utterly neglected to attend to them."

3. "He has refused to pass other laws for the accommodation of large districts of people, unless those people would relinquish the right of representation in the legislature, a right inestimable to them, and formidable to tyrants only."

4. "He has called together legislative bodies at places unusual, uncomfortable, and distant from the depository of their public records, for the sole purposes of fatiguing them into compliance with his measures."

5. "He has dissolved representative houses repeatedly and continually for opposing with manly firmness his invasions on the rights of the people."

6. "He has refused for a long time after such dissolutions to cause others to be elected, whereby the legislative powers, incapable of annihilation, have returned to the people at large for their exercise, the state remaining in the mean time exposed to all the dangers of invasion from without and convulsions within."

7. "He has endeavored to prevent the population of these States; for that purpose, obstructing the laws for naturalization of foreigners, refusing to pass others to encourage their migrations hither, and raising the conditions of new appropriations of lands."

8. "He has suffered the administration of justice totally to cease in some of these States refusing his assent to laws for establishing judiciary powers."

9. "He has made our judges dependent on his will alone, for the tenure of their offices, and the amount and payment of their salaries."

10. "He has erected a multitude of new offices by a self-assumed power and sent hither swarms of new officers to harass our people and eat out their substance."

11. "He has kept among us in times of peace standing armies and ships of war without the consent of our legislatures."

12. "He has affected to render the military independent of, and superior to the civil power."

13. "He has combined with others to subject us to a jurisdiction foreign to our constitutions and unacknowledged by our laws, giving his assent to their acts of pretended legislation

for quartering large bodies of armed troops among us; for protecting them by a mock-trial from punishment for any murders which they should commit on the inhabitants of these States; for cutting off our trade with all parts of the world; for imposing taxes on us without our consent; for depriving us of the benefits of trial by jury; for transporting us beyond seas to be tried for pretended offences; for abolishing the free system of English laws in a neighboring province, establishing therein an arbitrary government, and enlarging its boundaries so as to render it at once an example and fit instrument for introducing the same absolute rule into these States; for taking away our charters, abolishing our most valuable laws, and altering fundamentally the forms of our governments, for suspending our own legislatures, and declaring themselves invested with power to legislate for us in all cases whatsoever."

14. "He has abdicated government here withdrawing his governors, and declaring us out of his allegiance and protection."

15. "He has plundered our seas, ravaged our coast, burnt our towns, and destroyed the lives of our people."

16. "He is at this time transporting large armies of foreign mercenaries to complete the works of death, desolation and tyranny already begun with circumstances of cruelty and perfidy unworthy and head of a civilized nation."

17. "He has constrained our fellow citizens taken captive on the high seas to bear arms against their country, to become the executioners of their friends and brethren, or to fall themselves by their hands."

18. "He has endeavored to bring on the inhabitants of our frontiers the merciless Indian savages, whose known rule of warfare is an undistinguished destruction of all ages, sexes, and conditions of existence."

19. "He has incited, treasonable insurrections of our fellow-citizens, with the allurements of forfeiture and confiscation of our property."

20. "He has waged cruel war against human nature itself, violating its most sacred rights of life and liberty in the persons of a distant people who never offended him, captivating and carrying them into slavery in another hemisphere or to incur miserable death in their transportation thither, this piratical warfare, the opprobrium of infidel powers is the warfare of the Christian king of Great Britain. determined to keep open a market where Men should be bought and sold, he had prostituted his negative for suppressing every legislative attempt to prohibit or to restrain this execrable commerce, and that this assemblage of horrors might want no fact of distinguished die, he is now exciting those very people to rise in arms among us, and to purchase that liberty of which he has deprived them, by murdering the people on whom he also obtruded them; thus paving off former

crimes committed against the liberties of one people, with crimes which he urges them to commit against the lives of another." "In every stage of these oppressions we have petitioned for redress in the most humble terms; our repeated petitions have been answered only by repeated injuries. a prince whose character is thus marked by every act which may define a tyrant is unfit to be the ruler of a people who mean to be free, future ages will scarcely believe that the hardiness of one man adventured, within the short compass of twelve years only, to lay a foundations so broad and so undisguised for tyranny over a people fostered and fixed in principles of freedom.

Nor have we been wanting in attentions to our British brethren, we have warned them from time to time of attempts by their legislature to extend a jurisdiction over these our States. We have reminded them of the circumstances of our emigration and settlement here, no one of which could warrant so strange a pretension; that these were effected at the expense of our own blood and treasure, unassisted by the wealth or the strength of Great Britain; that in constituting indeed our several forms of government, we had adopted one common king, thereby laying a foundation for perpetual league and amity with them; but that submission to their parliament was no part of our Constitution, nor ever an idea, if history may be credited; and we appealed to their native justice and magnanimity as well as to the ties of our common kindred to disavow these usurpations which were likely to interrupt our connection and correspondence, they too have been deaf in the voice of justice and of consanguinity, and when occasions have been given them by the regular course of their laws. Of removing from their counsels, the disturbers of our harmony, they have by their free election, re-established them in power, at this very time too they are permitting their chief magistrate to send over not only soldiers of our common blood, but Scotch and foreign mercenaries to invade and destroy us. These facts have given the last stab to agonizing affection and manly spirit bids us to renounce for ever these unfeeling brethren, we must endeavor to forget our former love for them, and to hold them as we hold the rest of mankind, enemies in war, in peace friends. We might have been a free and a great people together; but a communication of grandeur and of freedom it seems is below their dignity. be it so since they will have it, the road to happiness and to glory is open to us too, we will tread it apart from them and acquiesce in the necessity which denounces our separation.

We therefore the representatives of the United States of America in General Congress assembled do in the name, and by the authority of the good people of these States reject and renounce all allegiance and subjection to the kings of Great Britain and all others who may hereafter claim by, through or under them; we utterly dissolve all political connection which may heretofore have subsisted between us and the people or parliament of Great Britain; finally we do assert and declare these colonies to be free and independent States and that as free and independent States, they have full power to levy war; conclude peace, contract alliances, establish commerce, and to do all other acts and things which independent States may of right do and for the support of this declaration we mutually pledge to each other our lives, our fortunes and our sacred honour." There were quite a few changes made, the biggest being the elimination of numbers Nineteen and Twenty dealing with slavery. Also, some general language changes. It has been reported that the Declaration was the original work of Jefferson's, but of course all five on the committee worked on it. In the politics of the second Continental Congress, it was Adams that rose and pushed it through.

John Adams went home to retirement following the second Continental Congress. He was asked and given a commission as a diplomat and sent to Europe to help in getting funding for the war. His son and sixth future president went with him. John wanted him with him so he would get diplomatic experience.

John Adams, Henry Laurens, John Jay, and Benjamin Franklin worked on a treaty to end the war known as "the treaty of Paris", negotiating with Great Britain on the one side and the American Colonies, France, Spain, and the Dutch republic on the other. Unfortunately, Spain didn't want peace until it captured Gibraltar. The deal they settled on was to give us independence with the territory from the Appalachians east, south of the Ohio river with an independent barrier state and to the north of Spanish Florida.

John Jay, part of our American contingent, believing they could do better, asked for direct talks with England, which they got. England wanting to split off America from France, they signed a treaty giving us independence with holdings as far west as the Mississippi following the present Canadian border and north of Spanish Florida.

He served as a diplomat trying to get treaties of commerce, and eventually became a minister to England. He returned home after ten years abroad. By now the Constitutional Convention was behind us. George Washington was elected president with Adams being his vice-president, a job he thought useless, no worse a job any republic had ever created. As president of the Senate, he broke tie votes siding with the Federalist policies of the day.

During the campaign of 1796, only Aaron Burr campaigned, but a lot of dirt was swung by his supporters. Jefferson was called an atheist, and Adams accused of wanting to set up a monarchy with his son. Adams barely won by three votes. Mostly on lines north and south with two votes from Virginia and North Carolina giving him the presidency. It is the only time we had a president of one party and vice president of another, unless you want to call Lincoln's re-election with a Democrat and Republican running on the Union ticket. He was sworn in by the Chief Justice of the supreme court Oliver Ellsworth and he retained Washington's cabinet appointees. He was a free-thinking man making decisions without input from his administration and had an administration free of personal scandals. Through the course of his presidency, things got decisive politically and he only served one term. After his loss in 1800 which was a very bitter campaign, he left town not even attending Jefferson's inauguration.

When the French Revolution broke out, the Republicans under Jefferson supported them vehemently with Hamilton and Adams favoring England. He stayed Washington's course of keeping America out of war even when our ships were seized. Americans were outraged and he sent a peace delegation to France.

In arguing for neutrality during what amounts to a state of the union address he states that, "Although it is very true that we ought not to involve ourselves in the political system of Europe, but to keep ourselves always distinct and separate from it if we can…It is necessary, in order to the discovery of the efforts made to draw us into the vortex, in season to make preparations against them…It would not only be against our interests, but it would be doing wrong to one-half of Europe, at least, if we should voluntarily throw ourselves into either scale." His greatest accomplishment is in keeping us out of war, I'm sure not an easy accomplishment at the time. And when our delegation arrived in France, they refused to meet with them without first paying a bribe. Our delegation was asked to sign on lines XYZ, which became known as the XYZ Affair, which really outraged the American people.

He also orders the mint to begin making coinage for circulation, thereby making foreign coins unusable, other than that of Spanish, to be made legal tender throughout the States. After the passing of the Alien and Sedition Acts, there was nothing of greater importance here, and the Federalist party lost favor among the people, and he lost in the election of 1800 to Jefferson.

On July 4th, 1826, just fifty years after the declaration of independence, he died just a few hours after Jefferson, his last thoughts being of him stating" Thomas Jefferson still survives."

Quotes taken from private letters to Abigail Adams. Original language of the Declaration taken originally from *The Papers of Thomas Jefferson Vol. 1: 1760-1776 by Julian P. Boyd*. Speech before the house taken from *The Compilation of the Messages and Papers of the Presidents*.

CHAPTER 14
ALIEN AND SEDITION ACTS STATES RESPONSE

During the Adams administration and following the French Revolution, war broke out between England and France. Our country was divided on the issue primarily along party lines, many writers were arguing in papers on behest of one or the other. Adams kept us out of the war and neutral, it is considered one of his greatest accomplishments. In other words, he kept the neutrality plank from Washington's administration, however laws were passed dealing with the effects of hostilities. The law "The Alien Act" passed in 1798 which "authorized the president to order out of this country all such aliens as he might judge dangerous to peace and safety of the United States." The Alien Act lengthened the eligibility from five to fourteen years to become a citizen. The Sedition Act targeted those opposing the governmental policies. At the time, this would mean anyone writing editorials criticizing the Federalists in power. Clearly going too far and the main reason there is no Federalist party to this day.

Obviously, this was in direct violation of the First Amendment which was added to the Constitution in 1792. The Republican party led by Jefferson found these laws to be unconstitutional. Today we would run to the Supreme Court, but prior to the "Marbury vs Madison" decision in 1803, there had been no judicial review as there is today. So, there was no way to find it unconstitutional.

Jefferson and Madison's solution was to try and void law through the State's legislatures. They wrote and passed the Kentucky and Virginia resolutions and then had them sent to other States. In them, they argue that there is a compact between the States and the federal government due to the Constitution, and when the federal government passes laws that are in violation of that compact with the federal government, they can simply void them through the States.

The resolutions were actually written in secret, because in writing them, they could become a foul of the "Sedition Act" itself.

Jefferson, in writing in the Kentucky resolution of 1798, begins by stating "that the several States composing, the Unites States of America, are not united on the principle of unlimited submission to their general government; but that, by a compact under the style and title of a Constitution for the United States, and of amendments thereto, they constituted a general government for special purposes," and then goes on to point out those purposes, and throughout the resolutions, continually points out the language of the tenth amendment restricting the federal government, not the States.

In Kentucky's 1799 resolution it states "resolved that this commonwealth considers the federal union, upon the terms and for the purposes specified in the late compact, as conductive to the liberty and happiness of the several States; that is does not unequivocally declare its attachment to the union, and to that compact, agreeable to its obvious and real intention, and will be among the last to seek its dissolution;" they are hereby advocating succession for the purpose of erecting a new government, or at the very least instructing the federal government that they have that right.

Madison writing for Virginia states "that this assembly doth explicitly and peremptorily declare, that it views the powers of the federal government, as resulting from the compact, to which the States are parties; as limited by the plain sense and intention of the instrument constituting the compact; as not further valid that they are authorized by the grants enumerated in that compact; and that in case of a deliberate, palpable and dangerous exercises of other powers, not granted by the said compact, the States who are parties thereto, have the right, and are in duty bound, to interpose for arresting the progress of the evil, and for maintaining within their respective limits, the authorities rights and liberties appertaining to them....That this state having by its Convention, which ratified the federal Constitution, expressly declared, that among other essential rights, "The liberty of conscience and of the Press cannot be cancelled, abridged, restrained, or modified by any authority of the United States." and finishes by ordering this resolution sent to every State and federal elected official less the president himself.

These resolutions encompass the doctrine of nullification and secession, but the more important thing to note is the Republicans led by Jefferson took over both houses and the presidency in the election of 1800, this becoming a very big campaign issue and repealed the law which is what really becomes. I think, the best way to deal with this.

Nullification, secession, sanctuary cities interstate compacts or any other way to escape the law is a problem, I believe anyway. Ignoring the law doesn't change it and, in the end, unconstitutional or otherwise, inappropriate laws need to be either struck down, removed, or changed.

Chapter 15
Richard Dobbs Spaight Duelist

Richard Dobbs Spaight was born in New Bern North Carolina. He eventually became their first native-born governor. By the age of eight, he was orphaned and sent to live with his relatives in Ireland, where he attended the University of Glasgow.

When war broke out, he returned to the colonies and served as aid de camp to Major Richard Caswell and serving during the battle of Camden Court house, a major victory for the British. The British had come down and started a southern campaign in their mistaken belief that there were more loyalists in the south. He was elected as a delegate to the Continental Congress, serving in the North Carolina House of Commons, even selected as speaker.

He was part of the delegation sent to Philadelphia for the Constitutional Convention. While there, he wrote back asking for two more months of stipends as they felt the way others had brought wives and family that it would be quite a siege there.

The Governor, writing him personally, asking for an independent judiciary.

Finally, writing as a delegation at its conclusion what they thought were accomplishments of the convention, "Enclosed we have the honor to send you a copy, and when you are pleased to lay this plan before the General Assembly we entreat that you will do us the justice to assure that honorable body that no exertions have been wanting on our part," and going on, "We had many things to hope from a National Government and the chief thing we had to fear from such a Government was the risqué of unequal or heavy taxation, but we hope you will believe as we do," they talk about the Three-fifths clause as being an issue of taxation, and the return of fugitive slave guarantees, in contrast to giving up the power to regulate shipping and commerce. "It is expected a considerable share of the National Taxes will be collected by Import, Duties and Excises." After his return, he became a member of the State ratifying convention, speaking 11 times, but to no avail. They chose not to ratify it! Arguing before the assembly, "I am one of those that formed this Constitution. The gentleman say we exceeded our powers. I deny the charge." Among the accusations are the charges of forming an aristocracy, complaints of the ten-mile square for a federal government, under which they would regulate. He goes after the opposition as they try to tear it apart, arguing for ratification and still fails to get the job done. A year later it was adopted.

He ran unsuccessfully for governor and then senator. In 1792, following an absence for health issues, he was elected to the state house of representatives and then to governor. In 1798, he was elected to the US House of Representatives to fill a vacant seat, and later to a full term as a Federalist, but became disillusioned following "the Alien and Sedition Acts", during the Adams administration which gave wide powers in deporting and restraining people. He began to agree more and more with Jefferson and the Republicans and returned to State government as a Republican, calling for a repeal of the act.

He got involved in a heated campaign with a State legislator, Jon Stanly, with accusations of him being a traitor to his party, among other things, back and forth in published pieces in the Gazette, that is seems, they both paid for.

Eventually, demanding satisfaction, they met with their seconds Pasteur and Graham, fighting with flintlock smoothbore dueling pistols before an audience of several hundred people. The first shots missed, the second nicked the collar of his shirt and the audience begged for an end, but Spaight still demanded satisfaction. The third whizzed past his ear, but the fourth found its target hitting Spaight in his side. He succumbed to his wounds and died some twenty-three hours later, ending his long career in politics. Anti-dueling laws were passed. Stanly received a pardon, but lived to see two of his brothers die in duels. Some of our founders' traditions and ways may seem strange today, which is why I choose not to judge them by today's standards.

Taken from *The Records of the Federal Convention of 1787, The Debates On The Several Conventions, On The Adoption Of The Federal Constitution.*

Chapter 16
Benjamin Rush
Forgotten Father

Benjamin Rush was born in the township of Byberry fourteen miles from Philadelphia, now part of the city. His father passed away when he was about five years old, and his mother opened a store to help care for her children who numbered seven. He attended the college of New Jersey, now Princeton University, where he earned a Bachelor of Arts degree. He then apprenticed under Dr. John Redman of Philadelphia for five years and he convinced him to go to the best school at the time for medicine, the University of Edinburgh in Scotland. Benjamin Franklin helped finance his studies as he did for many young men.

He moved back to America and opened a practice and became a professor of chemistry. He was elected to the American Philosophical Society and wrote the first book in America on chemistry. Benjamin Franklin introduced him to a number of patriots which were in his inner circle, including Thomas Paine. He helped him write the pamphlet "Common Sense"; he suggested the title. Paine wanted to use the title "Plain Truth". He was also active in the Sons of Liberty, who were fighting to repeal the Stamp Act.

He was elected to the second Continental Congress and was influential in getting the Declaration of Independence signed. He had written a pamphlet on the importance of a declaration earlier.

In a letter to John Adams, he describes the scene of signing the Declaration this way, "Do you recollect the pensive and awful silence which pervaded the house when we were called up one after another, to the table of the president of Congress to subscribe what was believed by many at the time to be our own death warrants. The silence and gloom of the morning was interrupted. I will recollect only for a moment by Col. Harrison of Virginia who said to Mr. Gerry at the table 'I shall have the great advantage over you Mr.

Gerry when we are all hung for what we are now doing. From the size and weight of my body, I shall die in a few minutes, but from the lightness of your body you will dance in the air and hour or two before you are dead.' This speech procured a transient smile but was soon succeeded by the solemnity with which the whole business was conducted." You know, I never really thought of it in this way. The seriousness of it all, the long, sad, and sleepless nights over which they deliberated over this act which could find them all under the threat of a king's warrant. This letter discussing the scene is in a letter complaining on the way they were celebrating the 4th of July.

While serving in the army, he was appalled by the conditions of soldiers and especially the army hospitals. He tried to do something about it, writing letters, basically calling the leadership derelict in their duties, and he wrote an anonymous letter complaining about it and George Washington. Washington recognized his handwriting and when he questioned him about it, he resigned from the service. He later wrote a pamphlet on the medicine and care for the soldier's condition in the army. Which was used for nearly one hundred years as a manual for care of the soldier.

He was a big believer in bloodletting, the idea was to get rid of bad blood. Many people died due to his treatments, because they drained too much blood, including the father of our country. When he was on his death bed, he prescribed the same treatments for himself. He thought people got sick due to an imbalance in their own bodies and his theories created a large divide in medical theories.

He advocated for better treatment of the insane. He is known as the father of psychology. He became an avid abolitionist. He bought and held one slave for ten years and tried to get blacks into recruitment during a health epidemic. It was a somewhat common practice for abolitionists to buy slaves and later free them. He helped found the bible society of Philadelphia and was a big believer in the idea of natural rights, those given by God almighty.

Taken from *Adams Papers* a private letter from Benjamin Rush, July 20th, 1811.

Chapter 17
John Dickinson
Penman of the Revolution

John Dickinson is probably best remembered for a series of letters he wrote to the colonists, but he did much more. He served as a delegate from Delaware and a Philadelphia representative to the Continental Congress from Pennsylvania. A slaveholder from Delaware, he is the only slave-holding founder who managed to free his slaves in the early days of the Republic in 1777, and he became an avid abolitionist. Guided by his Quaker upbringing, he had private tutors. He studied under one who became Delaware's first Chief Justice, and he eventually studied law. He is known as the Penman of the Revolution.

Following the repeal of the Stamp Act, the King pushed through the Townshend Acts, a series of taxes, this is what he was writing against in the letters from a farmer in Pennsylvania. He begins by stating that "Being a master of my time, I spend a good deal of it in a library, which I think the most valuable part of my estate; being acquainted with two or three gentlemen of abilities and learning, who honor me with their friendship." I find it interesting how they all seem to write as if they're just common folks and this is no different. He does, however, get seriously into it soon enough. "If the BRITISH PARLIAMENT has a legal authority to order, that we shall furnish a single article for the troops here, and to compel obedience to that order; they have the right to order us to supply those troops with arms, clothes and every necessity, and to compel obedience to that order."

They're talking about the troops housed in the colonies. Britain was trying to get taxes to help pay for the seven-year war, known here as the French and Indian War, and frankly speaking, we were fighting what we saw as heavy taxation. "But the act now objected to, imposes duties on the British colonies; "to defray the expenses of defending, protecting and securing his majesty's dominion in America," and he goes on, "His majesty's dominions" comprehended not only the British colonies; but also the conquered provinces of Canada and Florida, and the British garrisons of Nova Scotia; for these do not deserve the name of colonies," so, here he points out that we are made to pay for all of North America including areas not in the colonies. They will not even "make an adequate provision for defraying the charge of the administration of justice and the support of civil government, in such provinces where it shall be "found necessary" and then signs off in one letter, "Oppose a disease at its beginning- A Farmer."

He continues to argue, and I think hammer his point home, that we should oppose all the Townshend acts as well as we had successfully forced the repeal of the Stamp Act! He even wrote the Liberty Song, a tune written to a popular song of the day and sung in bars and taverns all over. It could be argued it was America's first hit song.

He served in the Continental Congress, where he wrote both the "Olive Branch Petition", our last attempt at peace with Great Britain, and a document the King refused to even read, a fiery letter to the

King trying to make him understand that we were ready for war, if necessary, "The Declaration on the Causes and Necessities of Taking Up Arms". There were two versions written, one by Jefferson, but Congress chose his more fiery rendition. And in it, speaking of our forefather's settlement of the colonies he states, "an un-conquering spirit, they effected settlements in the distant inhospitable wilds of America, then filled with numerous and warlike nations of barbarians." He goes on about the original situation with England, "Societies of governments, vested with perfect legislatures were formed under charters from the crown, and a harmonious intercourse was established between the colonies and the kingdom from which they derived their origin." He wanted a resolution to the problem and wanted to stay with Britain, he was concerned over fighting the largest power on the planet and really tried to achieve some kind of settlement but was warning Britain that we were ready.

He wrote the first draft of the Articles of Confederation following his refusal to sign the Declaration of Independence. You see, he felt we weren't ready, he wanted unity. A more united colonies and alliances before we declared independence. While serving in the second Continental Congress when independence came up, many disagreed, but after Adams spoke, they were quite united, and he left the hall making himself absent from the meeting so it could be a unanimous vote.

The Articles of Confederation is a weak document as it gives too much power to the individual States, it just leaves them too much as independent states. However, from the end of the document it states, "And whereas it hath pleased the Great Governor of the World to incline the hearts of the legislatures we respectively represent in Congress, to approve of, and to authorize us to ratify the said Articles of Confederation and perpetual union." The perpetual union is what's important here.

He served as a delegate from Delaware to the Constitutional Convention, but became sick and was not there when signed, so one of the other signors wrote his name in. While there, he opposed the slave trade and moved to have slavery prohibited.

He served as an informal advisor to President Jefferson, and when he died, Jefferson heaped accolades upon his name.

When you look at each one, you can see why they all still matter to the fabric of our Republic, John Dickinson never wanted independence, he wanted a better situation and relationship with England.

Language I have used either comes from *Letters from a Farmer in Pennsylvania* originally published in the *Pennsylvania Chronicle and Universal Advertiser* or from *The Declaration of the Causes and Necessities of Taking Up Arms.*

Chapter 18
Pierce Butler
Life in Contradiction

Pierce Butler, Irish born, the son of Sir Richard Butler. An aristocrat who was a member of Irish Parliament. He was the third son born in his family, and because of this, he would not inherit his father's estate. Which is why his father bought him a commission in the British Army.

Most sons of prominence in this period either went into military service or to the clergy. He was sent to fight in America during the French and Indian War in which Britain won Canada from France. During this whole period, it seems anyway, that Great Britain and France were always in open hostility. One of the reasons why they became our ally. Pierce became stationed in Nova Scotia after he transferred to a new unit and was sent down to Boston during hostilities in the colonies. In fact, it was his regiment that was involved in the shooting of protesters in March 1770. In the event known as the Boston Massacre, when the troops fired into the crowd.

A year after the incident, he married Polly Middleton a daughter of a wealthy plantation owner in South Carolina. When his unit was sent back to England, he sold his commission and went to South Carolina. By this time, he had earned the rank of major in the British army.

In South Carolina, he bought a plantation, eventually making it through land purchases over the years into the largest plantation in the State. He even had a fleet of ships he used in his business ventures. His father-in-law and brother served in the patriot cause being elected to the first Continental Congress, the other being a signor of the Declaration. He was first elected in 1776 to the South Carolina legislature, a seat he held until the new Constitution was in place.

John Rutledge Governor had him help to organize defenses and he served in the position of brigadier general. The British, having been tied up in the north and decided through a lack of hostilities in the south that there must be loyal subjects, they began a southern strategy. Basically, they would start in Georgia and one by one take over the southern colonies. Butler, overseeing the state militias, helped to organize them, but they were no match for crack British troops. He fled the city of Charleston during what's known as the Siege of Charleston, many that were held prisoner were off the coast on a prison ship. He then helped to launch a counteroffensive. With his ships smashed and plantation destroyed, he was forced to seek loans in Europe and went over there looking after new markets. Upon his return, he attempted to reconcile with former loyalists and argued heavily for internal peace.

He was sent by his State as a delegate to the Constitutional Convention where he became probably it's largest pro-slavery advocate. He was very concerned about the issue of representation and rose many times. Arguing for slavery being equally counted, "The labour of slaves in S. Carolina was as productive and valuable as that of a freeman in Massachusetts that as wealth was the great means of defense and utility to the nation they were equally valuable to it with freeman; and that consequently an equal representation ought to be allowed for them in a government which was instituted principally for the protection of property and was itself to be supported by property," this being part of his motion for equal representation in Congress. There is also this, which I think best explains the 20-year moratorium on ending slavery in the Constitution, "the security of the southern states want is, that their negroes may not be taken from them, which some gentlemen within or without doors, have a very good mind to do." It's this fear by the southern states, that leaves intact this, I think anyway, a disgusting institution. In looking at our founders, they all had different views coming from diverse backgrounds, all working together for one common purpose, that being one of self-government and liberty!

In letters, he wrote of the Convention this way, "I could not refuse the last appointment of acting as one of their commissioners to the Convention to be held at Philadelphia, no doubt you have heard of the purport of the meeting, - to form a stronger Constitution on strict Federal principles, for the government, of the whole- I hope we may succeed. Our country expects much of us. We have sat every day since the 25th of May till last Saturday when we adjourned for one week.... We in most instances took the Constitution of Britain, when in its purity, for a model and surely, we could not have a better. We tried to avoid what appeared to us the weak parts of ancient as well as modern republics. How well we succeeded it is for you and other learned men to determine." He goes on to explain the basic divisions of the document. The Constitution, he writes, "I think will be agreed to and be adopted tho' it has some few opponents. Where is that work of man that pleases everybody!"

Following ratification, he was not a member of the ratifying convention, he served three terms as U.S. Senator, each time as a member of a different party, first as a Federalist, then a Republican, and finally, an independent.

His plantation was a near fortress off on the St. Simons Island. His plantations had immense security. Gated and guarded, he ruled his plantations like the general he'd been, a tyrant, slaves weren't even allowed to talk with each other, constantly riding up and down his great estate issuing orders. It was this environment that attracted Aaron Burr, a fugitive from justice following the duel involving Alexander Hamilton, he probably felt safe there operating under the name of Roswell King. It is this arrangement with Burr that eventually ended his career.

He retired living in Philadelphia, occasionally checking his southern estates, owning lands in various States. He died there and is interred in Christ Church Burial Ground in Philadelphia, along with a number of the other founders.

Quotes taken from the *Records of the Federal Convention of 1787* by Max Farrand.

CHAPTER 19
GOUVERNEUR MORRIS PENMAN OF THE CONSTITUTION

Franklin may have to have been carried into the convention hall, but Gouverneur Morris hobbled in due to a carriage accident he had at age 28. He fell while getting into a carriage, slipping, getting his legs caught between the spokes of the wheels and breaking his leg in several places. The doctor he saw told him he'd have to amputate and from then on, he looked like a pirate with his peg leg. The stories of his womanizing are legendary, it's believed he was fleeing a husband possibly at the time.

He served as ambassador to France replacing Jefferson, and at the time, he had a clear window to the revolution in France and kept journals of the ongoing terror there. He was considered a very good-looking man constantly chasing after women, and his body was used as a double while in France to carve a statue of George Washington.

His most important contribution is that of being on the committee of style, who turned the Constitution into a workable document, and he penned much of it, including the preamble, "We the people in order to form a more perfect union establish justice..." He had a long-storied career in government.

He was born into a wealthy New York family with vast holdings. His mother turned over their property for the British to use during the war in which they used as their headquarters. She was a loyalist and his brother served in the British army as even he did for a while, he joined a special militia unit operating in New York, but left when they refused to become part of the continental army. He could have easily avoided military service altogether as he was handicapped due to a childhood accident.

He became a member of the provincial Congress and worked on getting New York to become an independent colony. He also served as a member of the committee of safety. He couldn't serve in a new legislature that was set up because his home was in occupied territory at the time, but he did serve as a delegate to the Continental Congress. While there, he inspected the troops, finding them woefully unsupplied and in tatters, and worked to get help from Congress. He failed in his re-election to Congress from New York, and that is the reason why he moved to Philadelphia.

It is here that he became a delegate to the Constitutional Convention from that State. Arguing many times, he made more speeches that anyone while there on a variety of positions. It is here that he is arguing against equal representation. He thought of westerners as backwoodsmen without importance to the Republic "I suggest to you in time the western people would outnumber the Atlantic States I wish therefore to put it in the power of the latter to keep a majority of votes in their own hands. If the legislature is left at liberty, they will never readjust the Representation." I am sure this comes from his experiences with those living deep in the back country, but today we know through the prism of history that his concerns really had no merit.

It's the same as those arguing for slavery. Morris was a devoted abolitionist as you'll soon see, "I would never concur in upholding domestic slavery. It is a nefarious institution -It is the curse of heaven on the states where it has prevailed." From there, goes on to explain the different regions of the States, "Proceed southwardly, and every step you take thro' ye great regions of slaves, presents a desert increasing with ye increasing proportion of these wretched beings. Upon what principle is it that the slaves shall be computed in the representation? Are they men? Then make them citizens and let them vote? Are they property? Why then is no other property included? The houses in this city are worth more than all the wretched slaves which cover the rice swamps of South Carolina."

At the end, before signing, he cites that "the present plan as the best that was to be attained, we should take it with all its faults. The majority had determined in its favor and by that determination we should abide. The moment this plan goes forth, all other considerations will be laid aside- and the great question will be, shall there be a national government or not?"

Language taken from *The Records of the Federal Convention of 1787* by Max Farrand.

Chapter 20
Robert Morris Financier of the Revolution

"We mutually pledge to each other our lives, our FORTUNES and our sacred Honour." and so ends the Declaration of Independence.

No one lived this more than Robert Morris, the wealthiest merchant in all the colonies, and by the end of his life he had been to debtor's prison.

A delegate to the second Continental Congress, He served on the "committee of trade", a secret committee working on the procurement of arms. Also serving on the marine committee and the committee of correspondence, in so doing, he was in charge overseeing the continental navy, which he himself had given many vessels and the important financing of the war. He eventually resigned his seat. He formed the bank of North America, our first national bank, and started by giving twenty-five thousand pounds to George Washington to outfit and supply the troops.

He was opposed to independence and voted against it, at first anyway. He believed we needed a new government if we were to swear off the old, that, and foreign alliances. This was July first, by the second, he absented himself, leaving the room, and when it came time to sign it, he added his name to the document, and in so doing, joined them all. Following the Declaration, he signed the Articles of Confederation.

He also is one of the few founders that never served during the revolution. He was too busy raising funds to fund the war effort. He had a large smuggling operation going on to evade the British, he had a network of agents around the colonies, and Europe in general, to procure gunpowder.

He was sent as a delegate from Pennsylvania to the Constitutional Convention. He was being considered to be elected as president of the Convention. Anytime one is in a first meeting of any group, always the first order of business is to elect someone to chair it. This task was thought to fall to either Morris or Washington.

Morris settled the matter by immediately taking to the floor and nominating George Washington for the position. In so doing, he averted a major debate on the issue. "Mr. Robert Morris informed the members assembled that by their instruction, and on behalf of the deputation of Pennsylvania, he proposed George Washington, esquire, late commander in chief, for president of the convention." Mr. Rutledge seconded the motion and it passed unanimously. George Washington stayed with him as a guest of his home.

Speaking of the Constitution, he states "This paper has been the subject of infinite investigation, disputation, and declamation. While some have boasted it as a work from Heaven, others have given it a less righteous origin. I have many reasons to believe that it is the work of plain, honest men, and such I think, it will appear, faulty it must be, for what is perfect? But if adopted, experience will, I believe show that its faults are just the reverse of what they are supposed to be. As yet this paper is but a dead letter... Adopt it which I hope and believe, there will then be little doubt of a general acquiescence." There isn't much else to say as he nearly, if ever, spoke in the Convention on any practical matter.

After the Convention, Washington offered him the position of Secretary of the Treasury, which he declined, and suggested the job to Alexander Hamilton. He became the first senator elected from Pennsylvania. He invested heavily in a land speculation company he was trying to recoup the loss from financing the war, but during our first financial panic, he went under, owing far more than he had and was sent to debtor's prison.

This is important because it caused Congress to pass bankruptcy laws. They couldn't allow him to stay in prison after all he had done for the young Republic. Following this, he retired from government, living out his years quietly.

This man helped appoint Washington as General and as president of the Convention, suggested Hamilton for Secretary of the Treasury, pushed for Jefferson to write the first draft of the declaration. He appointed, made people, understanding their abilities. Pushing men who would do a better job than himself. He gave it all for the good of the Republic, leaving nothing for himself!

CHAPTER 21
IN CONVENTION ASSEMBLED
THE VARIOUS PLANS

In western Virginia lies a trio of homes of our founders, three presidential homes. The grandest of all is "Monticello", Thomas Jefferson's beloved home, it lies at the top of a mountain. It's a modern home, even by today's standards. It has large, manicured lawns, beautiful flower-lined walkways, and brick terraces. It is truly magnificent. After he married, on his way home, a snowstorm began and increased to a blinding fury. He drove his carriage as far as he could in the blinding snow. Finally stopping, having to walk the rest of the way, while carrying his new bride. His home was a two-story building with a dome. It had a beautiful library for its day, eventually he donated it to the federal government. That became the beginning of the Congressional Library, after the burning of the white house.

Not far away, and even in sight on a clear day stands "Ash Lawn" Monroe's home and good friend of Jefferson's. He even sent his landscaper over to help him with a fine garden. His home was not elaborate, it looks more like a fine farmhouse.

A way off, but certainly within a drivable distance even by carriage, stands "Montpellier", the ancestral home of James Madison, known as Father of the Constitution. His wife Dolly Madison is famous for saving paintings while the White House burned in the war of 1812. She was truly our first modern First Lady. James Madison was a thin short man of 5' 4". He was modest, quiet, and always dressed in black, while his wife was quite outgoing. All these plantation homes housed numerous slaves; they were immensely large plantations in the traditions of the south.

On Feb 21, 1787, Congress approved a plan to send delegates to a national convention for the purpose of proposing amendments to the Articles of Confederation. Problems had existed since its adoption, issues of trade and taxation, the government simply wasn't strong enough to force compliance on nearly anything. Madison was selected as a Virginia delegate, his friend Jefferson was out of the country at the time, so was absent from these proceedings. Madison's home is quite large, and the formal entry overlooks a large, green space, probably running nearly a quarter mile. In his home, on the upper floor, is his library. From a large window, you can overlook his lawn. His is a busy estate with people coming and going all day. He spent the next several months combing through plans on self-government throughout the world, everything he could get his hands on, trying to develop an outline for a government plan for the new nation.

Away in Philadelphia, they were preparing for a meeting, which was held in the state house now known as Independence Hall. By May 14th, some delegates began to arrive. Madison had arrived early and was meeting with the other delegates, arguing for an all-new Constitution to replace the Articles of Confederation. He had a list of delegates and was organizing them on whether he thought they'd support him or not. It wasn't until the 25th when they had a working quorum and, on that day, they elected George Washington to be the president of the

Convention, there was debate on rules and the need for a whole new document versus simple amending of the Articles of Confederation. On May 29th two plans were proposed the first read by Mr. Randolph. It was the plan Madison had been working on, soon to be known as the Virginia plan.

The points are as follows.

1. That the Articles of Confederation ought to be so corrected and enlarged as to accomplish the objects proposed by their institution, namely, "Common defense, security of liberty and general welfare."

2. Legislature to be proportional to the quotas of contributions, or to the number of free inhabitants, one or the other.

3. The legislature is to consist of two branches.

4. The first branch to be elected by the people in each state. For the age and term to be decided, with compensation to be given for their services and to be ineligible for any state offices, except those belonging to the function

of the first branch. They shall be subject to recall and not eligible for office again for a time to be specified.

5. The second branch members to be elected out of the first branch. To be taken out of members of the state legislators, age to be decided; to hold their offices for a term sufficient to endure their independency; and a salary to compensate them for their service to be ineligible to any other public office, except those providing for the second branch for their years of service and for a space of time after the expiration of their term.

6. Congress would have the right to initiate acts and have the rights empowered to enjoy legislative rights vested in Congress by the confederation, to legislate where States are incompetent or where the United States would be in harmony. And to call forth the force of the union against any member of the union failing to fulfill its duty under these articles.

7. An executive to be chosen by the legislature for a specified term to receive a salary for their service which can't be changed and will not be eligible a second time. They will have the authority to execute laws and to enjoy the rights vested in the confederation.

8. The executive and a number of the judiciary which shall consist of a council of revision to examine laws before their operation. Their decision being final unless the legislature can vote again to override their decision.

9. A national judiciary established with a supreme and inferior courts to be chosen by the legislature to serve for life and receive a salary for their services for any issues of law, impeachments of national officers, and questions of national peace and harmony.

10. That a provision for the admission of States subject to the legislature.

11. A guarantee of a Republican form of government in each State.

12. A continuation of Congress until the approval of the articles of union.

13. The national legislature is not required for approval of the articles of union.

14. The legislative, executive and judiciary be bound by an oath to support the articles of union.

15. These amendments to be approved by assemblies of representatives, recommended by the state legislatures to be chosen by the people to consider and decide the issues.

As you read through each of these, you'll notice the many differences from which we now govern ourselves. This is due to the many changes they went through while working on them throughout the Convention. So, next is an outline put forth by Charles Pinckney of South Carolina. He was otherwise known as "Constitutional Charlie" as he would take to the floor on virtually everything. The original plan is missing, this draft being taken from James Wilson's notes, the copy Pinckney ultimately submitted in 1818 seems to contradict his arguments on the floor of the Convention, so it is much disputed. This is known going forward as the Pinckney Plan.

1. A Confederation between the free and independent states is hereby solemnly made uniting them together under one general superintending Government for their common benefit and for their defense and security against all designs and leagues that may be injurious to their interests and against all force and attacks offered to or made upon them or any of them.

2. The Style.

3. Mutual intercourse, community of privileges surrender of criminal faith to proceedings etc.

4. Two branches of the legislature, a House of Delegates and a Senate to make up a Congress. The House of Delegates to consist of one member for every number to be decided per thousand of inhabitants three fifths of blacks included.

The Senate to be elected from four districts, serving a rotation of four years to be elected by the House of Delegates from themselves or the people at large.

5. The Senate and House of Delegates by joint ballot to choose the President from themselves or the people at large annually. He shall be vested with the executive authority and have the right to advise with the heads of the different departments of his council.

6. Council of revisions consist of the President, Secretary of Affairs, War, heads of the Department of Treasury and Admiralty or any two of them together with the President.

7. Members of the Senate and the House shall each have one vote and be paid out of the common treasury.

8. Time of elections to be specified.

9. No State may make treaties, lay imposts, keep a military naval or land. Only a militia to be regulated by the United States.

10. Each State retains its rights not delegated. All laws must go through both branches of government before becoming law.

11. Exclusive powers of the house and Senate are in Congress.

12. Congress shall have the exclusive power to regulate trade and levy imposts, but each State may lay embargos in time of scarcity.

13. Establishing post offices.

14. The Senate and House of Delegates shall have the last authority in disputes between two or more States; the authority shall be exercised in the following manner.

15. The Senate and House of Delegates shall institute offices and appoint officers for the Departments of Affairs, War, Treasury and

Admiralty. They shall have exclusive power to declare what is treason and mishap of treason against the United States and of instituting a federal court to which an appeal shall be involved from the lower state courts in questions of construction of treaties made by the U.S. or on the law of nations or on regulations concerning trade and revenue. The court shall consist of judges to be appointed for life. Congress shall have the right of instituting in each state a court of Admiralty, appoint the judges and court of the same for all maritime cases.

16. Congress shall have the right of coining money, regulating the alloy and value, fixing the standards of weights and measures throughout the U.S.

17. Points in which the assent of more than a bare majority shall be necessary.

18. Impeachments shall be by the House of Delegates, before the Senate and the judges of the federal judicial court.

19. Congress shall regulate the militia.

20. Means of enforcing the quota and compelling the payment of each State.

21. Manners and conditions of admitting new States.

22. Power of dividing annexing and consolidating States, on the consent and petition of such States.

23. The assent of the legislature of the States shall be sufficient to invest future additional powers in the United States in Congress assembled and shall bind the whole confederacy.

24. The Articles of Confederation shall be inviolably observed, and the Union shall be perpetual unless altered as before directed.

There really is such a wow factor here especially in his view of constant elections, and the apparent weakness of the Presidency. And in the last two, you really have a doctrine of States' rights. The other thing

I find interesting is the great break in the Virginia plan away from the Articles of Confederation which they were supposed to be amending.

After the proposals of these two plans, it was decided to lay them side by side for a comparison. Then on June 15th, Mr. Patterson of New Jersey offered a plan to replace the Virginia Plan, which came to be known as the New Jersey Plan. Here it is for your review.

First- the Articles of Confederation had to be enlarged to render the federal Constitution adequate to the exigencies of government, to preserve the Union.

Second- in addition to congressional powers, they be authorized to pass acts for raising revenue, to regulate foreign and domestic commerce, provide for recovery of fines, to be in the common law judiciaries of the several States with an appeal.

Third- rules of apportioning taxation on the States shall be whites and three fifths of all others. If States are in arrears, Congress can pass laws to remedy the situation.

Fourth- Congress to appoint persons to be an executive in office with a fixed salary and ineligible a second time.

Fifth- executive to make judicial appointment during good behavior to try impeachments of federal officers and appeals from the state judiciary in all cases.

Sixth -the acts of treaties of federal law can be enforced by the executive.

Seven- that a provision be made for the addition of new States.

Eight - naturalization be the same in all States.

Nine- a citizen found guilty in one State is guilty in another.

Following these plans, Alexander Hamilton rose, not liking any of them, he lays out what he wants. Some call this the Hamilton Plan, but he, by his own admission, said he didn't have one. And from that point on, they worked off the Virginia Plan. All through the hot summer months, under an order of secrecy. They didn't want any information leaking out until they had finished. They worked in the hot hall, had meetings in their rented rooms in the city, and met for suppers trying not to discuss the particulars out in public. Like in anything though, there were times one delegate, or another, would slip up while on the town and be immediately reminded of their cause of secrecy. At one-point important copies of papers were found, that a delegate had dropped, and it was laid upon the desk for the delegate who had lost his copy to retrieve.

It should be noted how different these plans are. For instance, the Pinckney and New Jersey Plans had intended to keep much of the Articles of Confederation intact. While the Virginia Plan was meant to be a clean break and depart from it.

Their beliefs in natural law stem from their belief in the Almighty. In the open letter from "1802" earlier mentioned, it states a good example of what I'm talking about.

"But this systematic encroachment on natural rights-their abominable attempt to break down the few barriers, which nations have erected against the barbarous maxims of despotic will, and to revive the ancient savage rules of warfare, ought to be resisted by every civilized nation. Natural law permits no abridgement of the sovereignty, nor interruption of the commerce of any nation, without its consent- this is the high prerogative of compact only, and wretched will be our condition, if we cannot maintain the ground which has been gained by ancient treaties."

Weeks into the convention, Dr. Franklin rises to ask for prayer for the proceedings, citing the deadlock which they seem to be in. This falls in direct contradiction to the belief that this was not a religious nation. The reason this is important is because Jefferson and Franklin both were the lessor or least religious men among them.

"The small progress we have made after four- or five-weeks close attendance and continual reasonings with each other- our different sentiments on almost every question, several of the last producing as many nays as ayes, is methinks a melancholy proof of the imperfection of the human understanding. We indeed seem to feel our own want of political wisdom, since we have been running about in search of it, we have gone back to ancient history for more models of government and examined the different forms of those republics which having been formed with the seed of their own dissolution now no longer exist and we have viewed modern states all around Europe. But find none of their constitutions suitable to or circumstances… In the beginning of the contest with Great Britain when we were sensible of danger, we had daily prayer in this room for the Divine Protection. Our prayers,

Sir, were heard, and they were graciously answered… Have we not forgotten that powerful friend? Or do we imagine that we no longer need his assistance? I have lived Sir, a long time and the longer I live, the more convincing proof I see of this truth that God governs in the affairs of Men. And if a sparrow cannot fall to the ground without his notice, is it probable that an empire can rise without his aid?... I firmly believe this; and I also believe that without his concurring aid we shall succeed in this political building no better that the builders of Babel… I therefore beg to move, that henceforth prayers imploring the assistance of Heaven, and its blessings on our deliberation, be held in this assembly every morning before we proceed to business, and that one or more of the Clergy of this City be requested to officiate in that service."

Something more that needs to be understood, with the accusation that the Federalists wanted to institute some kind of aristocracy. All be it true that they were more pro-Britain than the Republicans were, they were not really for staying with the crown. Rufus King, speaking in convention as reported here, "young men who have been born since the revolution, look with horror upon the name of a King, and upon all propositions for a strong government. It was not so with us. We were born the subjects of a King, and were accustomed to subscribe ourselves "His majesties most faithful subjects," and we began the quarrel which ended in the Revolution, not against the King, but against his parliament; and in making the new government many propositions were submitted which would not bear discussion; and ought not to be quoted against their authors being offered for consideration, and to bring out opinions and which though behind the opinions of this day were in advance of those of that day."

This might seem like a minor distinction that they were not against the crown itself, but his parliament. Yet it is something to be noted that one would not really be divorced from the other!

These plans were taken from *The Records of The Federal Convention of 1787* by Max Farrand. I did change the wording to make it more readable to the casual reader.

CHAPTER 22
DECLARATION OF INDEPENDENCE

I think here I should add a little about the Declaration and the stormy times they were working under in 1776. It was proposed in the late spring and the committee working on it came back, and throughout the debate once the document was written, you could hear the storms, cannon fire, the sounds of revolution out in the distance. Jefferson sitting quietly, while they tore apart his document, debating it line after line, and with each State having only one vote; voting by State and with delegations arguing amongst themselves in order to cast their vote. Through all this debate, Adams stepped up, fighting in its defense to speak, notes were taken but no draft survives. What we do have is a rendition or reconstruction of his speech as put together by the great orator of the 19th century Daniel Webster. So, I'll include that here.

"Sink or swim, live or die, survive or perish, I give my hand and heart to this vote. It is true indeed, that in the beginning we aimed not at independence. But there is a divinity that shapes our ends. The injustice of England has driven us to take up arms, and blinded to our own interest for our good, she has ostensibly persisted, till independence is now within our grasp; We have but to reach forth to it, and it's ours, why then should we defer the declaration? Is any man so weak as to now hope for reconciliation with England, which shall leave either safety to the country, and its liberties, or safety to his own life and his honour? Are not you, sir, who sit in that chair, is not he, our venerable colleague near you, are you not both already the proscribed and predestined objects of punishment and vengeance? Cut off from all hope of royal clemency, what are you, what can you be, while the power of England remains, but outlaws? If we postpone independence, do we mean to carry on, or to give up the war? Do we mean to submit to the pressures of parliament, Boston Port, Bill and all?

Do we mean to submit, and consent that we ourselves shall be ground to powder, and our country and its rights shall be trodden down in the dust? I know we do not mean to submit. We never shall submit. Do we intend to violate that most solemn obligation ever entered into by men- that plighting before God of our sacred honour to Washington, when putting him forth to incur the dangers of war, as well as all the political hazards of the times. We promise to adhere to him, in every extremity, with our fortunes and our lives? I know there is not a man here, who would not rather see a general conflagration sweep over the land, or an earthquake sink it. Than on jot or title of that plighted fate fall to the ground. For myself having, twelve months ago in this place, moved you, that George Washington be appointed commander of the forces, raised or to be raised, for defense of American liberty, may my right hand forget her cunning, and my tongue cleave to the roof of my mouth, if I hesitate or waiver in the support I give. The war must then go on, we must fight it through and if the war must go on, why put off longer the Declaration of Independence? That measure will strengthen us, it will give us character abroad, the nations will then treat with us, which they never can do while we acknowledge ourselves subjects, in arms against our sovereigns. Nay, I maintain that England herself, will sooner treat for peace with us on the footing of independence, than consent than, by repealing her acts, to acknowledge that her whole context before us has been a course of injustice and oppression. Her pride will be less wounded by submitting to that course of things which now predestinates our independence, than by yielding the points in controversy to her rebellious subjects. The former she would regard, as the result of fortune, the later she would reveal as her own, deep disgrace, why then, why, then sir, do we not as soon as possible change this from a civil to a national war? And since we must fight this through, why not put ourselves in a state to enjoy all the benefits of victory, if we gain victory, if we fail it can be no worse for us, but we shall not fail, the cause will raise up the armies; the cause will create the navies. The people, the people, if we are true to them, will carry us, and we will carry themselves gloriously, through this struggle, I care not how fickle other people have been found. I know the people of these colonies, and I know that resistance to British aggression is deep and settled in their hearts and cannot be eradicated. Every colony indeed, has expressed his readiness to follow if we but take the lead. Sir the declaration will inspire the people with increased courage. Instead of a long bloody war, for the restoration of privileges, for redress of grievances, for charted immunities, held under a British king, set before them the glorious object of entire independence, and it will breathe into them anew, the breath of life. Read this declaration at the head of the army, every sword will be drawn from its scabbard, and the solemn vow uttered, to maintain it or to perish, on the bed of honour. Publish it from the pulpit; religion will approve it, and love of religious liberty will cling around it, resolved to stand with it, or fall with it. Send it to the public halls, proclaim it there, let them hear who heard the first roar of the enemy's cannon. Let them see it who saw their brothers and their sons fall on the field of Bunker Hill, and in the streets of Lexington and Concord, and the very walls will cry out in support.

Sir, I know the uncertainty of human affairs, but I see, I see clearly, through this day's business, you, and I, indeed, may rue it, we may not live to the time, when this declaration will be made good. We may die, die colonists, die slaves, die, it may be, ignominiously, and on the scaffold, be it so, be it so, if it be the pleasure of heaven that my country shall require the poor offering of my life, the victim shall be ready, at the appointed hour of sacrifice, come when that hour may. But while I do live, let me have a country, or at least the hope of a country, and that a free country.

But whatever may be our fate, be assured, be assured that this declaration will stand. It may cost treasure, and it may cost blood; but it will stand, and it will richly compensate for both, through the thick gloom of the present I see the brightness of the future as the sun in heaven. We shall make this a glorious, an immortal day. When we are in our graves, our children shall honour it. They will celebrate it with thanksgiving, with festivity, with bonfires with illumination. On its annual return they will shed tears, copious gushing tears, not of subjection of slavery, not of agony and distress, but of exaltation of gratitude, and of joy, sir, before God, I believe the hour has come. My judgment approves this measure, and my whole heart is in it, all that I have and all that I am, and all that I hope in this life, I am now ready here to stake upon it. And I leave off as I begun, that live or die, survive or perish, I am for the Declaration. It is my living sentiment and by the blessings of God, it shall be my dying sentiment, independence now, and independence forever."

Following the speech, they were more united than ever. Morris and Dickenson absented themselves by leaving the room so it could be by States a unanimous vote. This really is the story of our founders stepping aside, then later injecting themselves always for the good of the Republic. The declaration I see as the beginning of our Republic, it for sure was a long fight, but it's here we declare our independence from Great Britain and become a nation. Before that we were protesting, fermenting a rebellion, and taking to the streets in a more or less united front against what we saw as tyranny. The Continental Congresses were part of that, a supporting network per say, but we still were part of Ole England until we declared independence and left the union which had united us with England.

Following the declaration, we began forming a government, a loose affiliation of States known as "the Articles of Confederation". Generally, a weak document guaranteeing individual State sovereignty. One of the problems was there was no instrument to force the colonies to comply. We sent diplomats overseas to establish treaties and get help with the cause.

On and on so goes our story, our history.

Chapter 23
The Bill of Rights

So here I'll give you a few words on our Bill of Rights which came out of the first Congress, written by James Madison, probably the most loved section of our Constitution. This is the Bill of Rights, 17 of them as sent out of the House of Representatives. As you read through these, it gives you an idea of what they were thinking about. Including a right of conscience, even allowing someone of religious conscience not to serve in the armed forces of the United States. Madison started with nineteen of them, seventeen made it through the House. Some didn't make it through the Senate, others were combined or otherwise re-organized, but even still, it gives you an idea into what they saw as natural rights.

Monroe and Madison were both running for the same congressional seat, Madison won by promising a bill of right to be included in the Constitution through the amendment process.

He wrote it, proposed it, pretty much dogged all the other members in Congress to agree to it. He fought hard, when something was lost, he just carried on with the rest, carefully maneuvering them through Congress. His preamble to the preamble didn't make it. But it's here for your consideration.

"That all power is originally vested in, and consequently derived from the people."

"That government is instituted, and ought to be exercised for the benefit of the people, which consists in the enjoyment of life and liberty, with the right of acquiring and using property, and generally of pursuit and obtaining happiness and safety."

"That the people have an indubitable, unalienable, and indefeasible right to reform or change their government, whenever it be found avertable right to reform or change their government, whenever it be found adverse or inadequate to the purposes of its institution."

This was to be inserted just before the "We the People" language, the other amendments he saw them all as being interwoven throughout the Constitution. This, too, didn't make the light of day. Which is why they're listed following the original document as amendments.

The following is the original approved Bill of Rights as passed by the House of Representatives and sent to the Senate.

Congress of the United States

In the House of Representatives, Monday August 24th, 1789-Resolved by the Senate and House of Representatives of the United States of America in Congress assembled, two thirds of both Houses deeming it necessary that the following articles be proposed to the several States, as amendments to the Constitution of the United States; all, or any of which articles, when ratified by three fourths of the said legislatures, to be valid, to all intents and purposes, as part of the Constitution.

ARTICLES in addition to, and amendment of the Constitution of the United States of America, proposed by Congress and ratified by the legislatures of the several States, pursuant to the Fifth article of the original Constitution.

ARTICLE 1. After the first enumeration required by the first article of the Constitution, there shall be one representative for every thirty thousand, until the number shall amount to one hundred, after which the proportion shall be so regulated by Congress that there shall not be less than one hundred representatives nor less than one representative for every forty thousand persons, until the number of representatives shall amount to two hundred, after which the proportion shall be so regulated by Congress, that there shall not be less than two hundred representatives for every fifty thousand persons.

ART. 2. No law varying the compensation to the members of Congress shall take effect, until an election of representatives shall have intervened.

ART. 3. Congress shall make no law establishing religion, or prohibiting the free exercise thereof, nor shall the rights of conscience be infringed.

ART. 4. The freedom of speech, and of the press, and the right of the people peaceably to assemble and consult for their common good, and to apply to the government for a redress of grievances shall not be infringed.

ART. 5. A well-regulated militia, composed of the body of the people, being the best security of a free state, the right of the people to keep and bear arms shall not be infringed, but no one religiously scrupulous of bearing arms, shall be compelled to render military service in person.

ART. 6. No soldier shall in time of peace be quartered in any house without the consent of the owner, nor in time of war, but in a manner to be prescribed by law.

ART. 7. The right of the people to be secure in their persons, houses, papers and effects against unreasonable searches and seizures, shall not be violated; and no warrants shall issue, but upon probable cause supported by oath or affirmation, and particularly describing the places to be searched and the persons or things to be seized.

ART. 8. No person shall be subject, except in a case of impeachment, to more than one trial or one punishment for the same offence, nor shall be compelled in any criminal case, to be a witness against himself, nor be deprived of life, liberty or property, without due process of law, nor shall private property be taken for public use, without just compensation.

ART. 9. In any criminal prosecutions, the accused shall enjoy the right to a speedy and public trial, to be informed of the nature and cause of the accusation, to be confronted with the witnesses against him, to have compulsory process for obtaining witnesses in his favour, and to have the assistance of counsel for his defense.

ART. 10. The trial of all crimes except in cases of impeachment, and in cases arising in the land or naval forces, or in the militia when in actual service in time of war or public danger shall be by an impartial jury of the vicinage, with requisite of unanimity for conviction; the right of challenge and other requisite; and no person shall be held to answer for a capital or otherwise infamous crime, unless on a presentment or indictment by a grand jury; but if a crime be committed in a place in the possession of an enemy, or in which an insurrection may prevail, the indictment and trial may by law be authorized in some other place within the same state.

ART. 11. No appeal to the Supreme Court of the United States shall be allowed, where the value in controversy shall not amount to one thousand dollars; nor shall any fact triable by a jury according to the other course of common law, be otherwise re-examineable, than according to the rules of common law.

ART. 12. In suits at common law, the right of trial by jury shall be preserved.

ART. 13. Excessive bail shall not be required, nor excessive fines imposed, nor cruel and unusual punishment inflicted.

ART. 14. No State shall infringe the right of trial by jury in criminal cases nor the right of conscience, nor the freedom of speech, or of the press.

ART. 15. The enumeration in the Constitution of certain rights shall not be construed to deny or disparage others retained by the people.

ART. 16. The powers delegated by the Constitution to the government of the United States, shall be exercised as therein appropriated, so that the legislator shall never exercise the powers vested in the executive or judicial; nor the judicial the powers vested in the legislative or executive.

ART. 17. The powers not delegated by the Constitution nor prohibited by it to the States, are reserved to the States respectably.

Orders that the Clerk of this House do carry to the Senate a fair and engrossed copy of the said proposed articles of amendments and desire their concurrence."

When they left the Senate, they were down to twelve. Of those twelve, the last ten were adopted by the States, the second was passed later as the twenty-seventh amendment. The first is still lying-in wait. If ever adopted, it would greatly enlarge the size of the House of Representatives.

I think the other interesting thing here, too, is the proposed amendments restricted the States, which the finalized version does not, so in essence another bow to State rights is herein.

CHAPTER 24
OUR CONSTITUTION AS EXPLAINED BY THE AUTHOR

Speaking of the Constitution, for a while now, I have been bothered by people of influence constantly, both left and right, being inaccurate to the point that most people don't understand it.

With an emphasis on textualism, in other words, what the text says. With the knowledge of the founder's vision at the time. I have studied the Constitution for decades, reading many old, old books and I've gone through the records of the Federal Convention and the debates on the Constitution as well as the Federalist papers, the Constitution itself and the Declaration of Independence. I didn't intend this to be some dry history lesson of memorizing places and dates. I seek a true understanding of what has been promised us.

Our original Constitution, between "We the people" and the signatures covers a lot of ground. The Electoral College, House, Senate, judiciary, and the executive branch. Basically, I see it kind of like a blueprint for your home, only one of government. It restricts the federal government in many ways, dividing up power because our founders were skeptical at best of anyone achieving too much power. It keeps power for the States, States' rights, only giving certain powers to the federal government which they would need for a central government.

In 1787 the Continental Congress sent delegates to Philadelphia to work out problems with the Articles of Confederation. This is the meeting which became our Constitutional Convention. Members brought different plans for the government, the Virginia and Pinckney Plans being Madison's and Charles Pinckney's of South Carolina, and later on the New Jersey Plan. Most of the time they dealt with the legislative body as outlined in Article I sections 1-3. The result was two branches of the legislature, one each from the two main plans. This was the great compromise; they had really entered into a stalemate. The House, "The Peoples House" would be representing the population and the Senate would represent the States. Which is why state legislatures were choosing the senators.

Jefferson was the minister to France, so was absent during this important period. Upon his return, it's said he visited Washington, and in complaining about the Senate, specifically the fact that we have two distinct branches, not understanding why. Washington asked him why he put his tea in the saucer, and he responded, it was to cool it, and Washington said, that's why we have the two branches.

Today we look at it so differently, as to which party maintains power, but really it shouldn't be looked at in this light. The Seventeenth Amendment changed things, allowing for direct elections of the Senate. Each branch had different duties attached to them. In studying the Constitution, power is split up all over, as our founders didn't trust anyone having too much power.

The States wanted to maintain autonomy, too. Some wanted the House to choose the senators, some wanted elections every year. They made it so the House was up every other year, along with a third of the Senate, so it would act as a cooling chamber against the other. This division of power is why our Constitution has lasted so long. Our founders formed a constitution for the ages on purpose, wanting it to be perpetual, as they described it, which is why they allowed for amendments. It is truly the pride of our nation. One of our founders described it this way, "The House would be filled with commoners while the Senate would be more aristocratic."

So, in Article I, Section 2, we establish the House of Representatives by population, we give temporary numbers that the States will have in Congress and order a census for the purpose of taxation, and representation. The reason for taxation is so the federal government can pay salaries of the members. They didn't want the State paying wages, or any gift or emolument, as it's called given.

The census to follow was for representation, which is why they tell us who to count. This is for the purpose of redistricting, which is what we go through every ten years. So, why do we redistrict? The short answer is so each member represents the same basic number in Congress. People move in and out of States, some cities shrink while others grow, for instance, Chicago really shrank after the Great Chicago fire as citizens fled the city in fear. Mostly, cities grow in population.

The big problem with redistricting is how the lines are drawn. Eldridge Gerry, the governor for Massachusetts in 1812, signed a redistricting bill, with maps which were redrawn to his party's advantage. One district looked like the shape of a salamander, which is why we call redrawing lines for partisan reasons gerrymandering.

When you have districts heavily weighted one way or another, it guarantees who will most likely win, and that's the problem, it creates fewer competitive districts. This is a defect of man's inherent desire for power. It is not a flaw of the Republic. Our founders wanted free and fair elections and set up a system to guard against power hungry politicians, which is why you have so many checks and balances.

Article II, Section 1. establishes the executive branch which houses the president and the vice-president. It gives the qualifications for office being a naturally-born citizen, thirty-five-years of age and a resident for fourteen years.

This section also houses a way for electing them, this being the Electoral College. The Electoral College is made up of the same combined number of senators and house members representing that State in Congress. Electors are chosen by the State and cannot be made up of anyone holding an office of public trust. In other words, they must be common citizens.

Electors meet on the same date, choosing two, one for each office. It is cleaned up by the Twelfth Amendment, which requires them to be distinct in their choice for which office each is to be. During a presidential election, this is what you're actually voting for, not the president, but your state's set of electors. I don't think our founders intended them to be solely of one party or another as they are today.

There has been a move in recent years for bypassing the Electoral College in favor of a popular vote. Some States have entered into a compact which would throw their electors to whoever won the popular vote. This is unconstitutional. Article I section 10 forbids any State from entering into a compact with another.

The Electoral College is part of States' rights, it was meant to protect smaller States from larger ones. It's more of our founder's brilliance and vision.

Over time, the presidency has gained a lot of power much more than our founders ever intended. It has almost made him a king. He can be, however, challenged in court on constitutional grounds, when he overstates his authority, and it seems every president these days is under threat of impeachment. It takes Congress to declare war and fund it, even though he's commander and chief. He is required to enforce all laws equally; he cannot choose one over the other. He cannot write law by himself; all spending bills must start in the House of Representatives. So, an executive order, no matter how justified, cannot overrun Congress. It requires each branch to work together. A president that overruns his authority will be challenged in court. Many times, our presidents lose in court. They just believe they can go it alone.

In Article II Section 3, it requires that the laws of the United States be faithfully executed, this is the job of the president of the United States. It also requires him from time to time to report to Congress on the state of the union. "The State of the Union Speech" usually given in the beginning months of the new year was not meant to be for political purposes, it was supposed to be to report to Congress and give reasons and recommendations. These days, we even have a rebuttal, the Democrat or Republican response in which they rip whatever the president just said.

Lately, it has come to my attention that our citizens have a lack of understanding of impeachment. In Article I Section 2. it states the House of Representatives has the sole power of impeachments.

Impeachment is the formal bringing of charges. You can be impeached without being found guilty and removed. Article II Section 4. gives the reasons as being for treason, bribery or other high crimes and misdemeanors. And in Article III Section 3. it defines treason. Once the House has brought charges, it is brought to the Senate for a trial.

As defined in Article I Section 3. The Senate shall have the sole power to try all impeachments, explains the penalty as removal from office and the disqualifying from holding any further office. The Senate shall sit as jury and when the president is tried, the chief justice shall preside. If nothing else, this section on impeachment really shows the separation of powers as it is serious enough to bring all three branches together deciding the issue.

There's always a drive for change due to a want of more power, some arguing recently of an inherent constitutional flaw. That being a flaw of the difficulty of amending it. Congress can send amendments to the States with two thirds vote of both houses of Congress, and then it requires three fourths of the States to ratify. I certainly don't dispute its difficulty, but it has been done twenty-seven times. Our prohibition against alcohol and then repeal shows you why it shouldn't be easier. You can imagine how long our document would be if it was an easy thing. Probably thousands of pages by now. The reason for this is so nearly all, a super majority, would agree on the changes. They also allowed for States calling for a convention of States for this same purpose. Giving States the right to call a meeting for such a purpose of proposing amendments but writing under the pseudonym of "Publius", our founders warned us about another meeting. Once you've started a meeting, everything could be up for grabs, anything could change.

In discussing our amendments, The Bill of Rights, or the first ten amendments, gives us specified freedoms and rights, but just because something isn't enumerated doesn't mean your restricted from it. Our

First Amendment lists two freedoms, that of press and speech. If we burn or ban books, the net result is more people want to see whatever is banned.

When people try to restrict political speech, it may not be discussed, but that really doesn't help, discussion and debate help to resolve the issue. It helps people to better understand each other.

Fact checking is not the best either, because your subject to what the fact checker thinks and their biases. Kicking people off platforms and firing people does nothing to resolve anything, it just shows hate for an opinion, the way to fight is not limiting speech, but accelerating the amount of it.

That's why we have the freedoms, it's easy to say what everyone already thinks already, but that's not free speech, saying what is unpopular is the reason for it. It allows dissent in a democratic republic, it's what is necessary. Likewise, press or the printed word allows people to enter the political arena as well, which is exactly why I wrote my book.

Freedom of press and speech are fundamental and why our founders insisted on them. Freedoms are not absolute, you don't have the right to slander people, for instance, but no one has the right to silence you either.

Our First Amendment doesn't just cover the freedom of press and speech. What we didn't talk about was the third plank of the First Amendment, that being of the right to practice religion. So why was that so important? It had to do with the reason for coming to America in the first place. It wasn't just the pilgrims, Irish and English Catholics were here, Presbyterians, Lutherans, followers of Calvin and a number of others.

England had the Catholic church, so they had a state-sanctioned religion, which is why they didn't want an established church here, that's why Congress was restricted from doing so.

As you read the Constitution, it didn't restrict the States, but did give a right to a free practice, eliminating government interference. It was never meant that people couldn't practice religion on government property, as some would argue today. It's really not so much a separation of church and state. It's allowing people to practice wherever they choose, however they choose, it's none of government's business. The Constitution restricts the federal government, States gave up some power so that the federal government could do what was necessary but reserved the rest to the States and the people thereof. Basically, inside a church synagogue, mosque, or other religious house, you have a sort of autonomy.

In the preamble it states, "We the people...Provide for a common defense..." In Article I Section 8, it gives Congress the authority to raise armies and to declare war. It's true the declaration of war is really a formality once hostilities begin, because at that point, we're already in a state of war, whether we like it or not.

In Article II Section 2, it makes the president commander-in-chief of the army, navy and the militia when called into service. States are restricted from keeping an army, but in Article I Section 10, it allows for States to defend themselves in cases of invasion, for instance, until the federal government intervenes.

So, what's this all have to do with the Second Amendment you might ask? We'll the amendment states, and I quote, "a well-regulated militia being necessary for the security of a free state, the rights of the people to keep and bear arms, shall not be infringed."

A security of a free State means we're talking about self-defense. The nation's self-defense, not hunting, or even personal self-defense. Although I admit, in 1792, out on the frontier, they were worried about possible uprisings.

The argument that is always brought up is as if it's for hunting. A one-shot black powder musket, which was typically all that was available at the time, we tend to conveniently forget, I think, that in 1792, this was a state-of-the-art weapon. Furthermore, the amendment gives the right to the people as a militia. The Supreme Court has ruled that a militia is every able-bodied man between the ages of 18 and 60. It's not a National Guard unit, the founders didn't trust standing armies because there are times you have to wonder throughout history which side the armies are on. Many of our founders served in the militia, sometimes referred to as minutemen as those men could be ready quickly. This right exists for the defense of the Republic period.

The Third Amendment is almost a lost amendment, but at the time of its passage, it was considered one of the most important. It reads "No person shall in time of peace be quartered in any house, without the consent of the owner, nor in time of war, but in a manner prescribed by law."

So, what are we talking about here? Well, following the French and Indian war, British troops stayed behind and there weren't enough places to house them, so parliament passed a law requiring the colonists to house them, they were trying to quell the riots by the patriots fighting against the Stamp Act, then the Townshend Acts, leading up to the war.

Imagine if you will, soldiers living in your home, basically spying on you. The Declaration, in complaints 11-13, if you were to number the complaints, talks about this and mock courts set up to let soldiers who had killed colonists go.

Today, people have the attitude like, "that couldn't happen here," but there are other examples of this very thing happening, usually by an occupying force for instance, in World War II during the occupation of Paris. Germany occupied homes using them for offices. In order to understand our rights, we need to know the originalist intent behind them!

Amendments IV - VIII taken together really all are encompassing the rights of the accused, guaranteeing a right to a jury trial, and denying double jeopardy, being tried twice for the same crime. The right against self-incrimination, you can't be forced to be a witness against yourself.

That you'll be secure in your own home and papers demanding probable cause in issue of a warrant and any warrant must be specific in what will be searched and seized and stating you can't be denied life liberty or property without due process of law.

In other words, you have to be found guilty. It also demands no excessive bail will be brought, that which under normal circumstances could not be paid and a moratorium against unreasonable or otherwise cruel or unusual punishment.

When taken together, it basically means you can't be punished for a crime unless you are proven guilty and guarantees that justice be blind, that you are innocent until proven guilty.

These are the amendments usually questioned in court, questioning whether an officer had the right to do this or that. Members of law enforcement are just employees, usually of the municipality, State, or other jurisdictional authority and that can become a problem if for instance the governing authority wants to ignore certain laws. The reason for these amendments goes all the way back to British law, where you have to be proven innocent, something almost impossible to do. So, our founders tried to remedy the situation.

The Ninth Amendment not often cited is the enumeration clause saying just because these rights are enumerated or numbered does not mean other rights are not included.

This goes back to Natural rights those given by God, the Constitution restricts the federal government, if it's not listed or denied to you, then you have the right under the Constitution. There are a number of things not defined that say, the Supreme Court has ruled on some things which clearly do not belong to the federal government.

This should be taken the same as with the Tenth Amendment which states, "The powers not delegated to the United States by the Constitution, nor prohibited by it to the States, are reserved to the States respectably or to the people." Basically, it gives States the rights not defined or restricted here. So, States are allowed to pass their own laws, basically giving them a certain amount of independence and autonomy to the federal government. So long as they don't trample on the rights given to the federal government, of course.

There are a number of things not talked about in the Constitution, so those things are up to the State, like say traffic laws, regulations of TV, radio, internet for instance, I am sure you can think of things far more important than that, however, everything is NOT the business of the federal government! That is to mean that they cannot support or restrict it, but surely your state government can.

Which brings us to the Twenty-seventh Amendment. I am skipping the others for now so that all the passed Bill of Rights are together. This is the last amendment to be adopted. Basically, if Congress gives itself a raise, it won't occur until after the next congressional election, thereby giving the people a chance to weigh in.

The Eleventh Amendment restricts the federal judiciary from weighing in on lawsuits between a citizen of one State, suing another State in court or a foreign national doing the same.

One of our earliest Supreme Court cases Chisholm vs Georgia, was a 4-1 decision finding against the State, the State never defended itself believing the Supreme Court had no standing. Chisholm had sued the State of Georgia for debts owed him due to goods received dealing with the war for independence.

Following the ruling, Congress sent a proposed amendment to the States to reverse the opinion. It was passed quickly to become part of the Constitution. This is a good example of the proper procedure of a case much disputed by the people.

That brings us to the election of 1796 and the pursuing constitutional amendment. The Twelfth Amendment dealt with the fact that under the Constitution, a flaw was found which allowed the executive branch to have divided power against itself. With the top vote-getter for president being of one party and the next highest being the vice-president and the leader of the other party. In a two-party system they would be opposing parties. As the Constitution stated, the highest number of votes would be the president's and the next highest, the vice-presidents.

In this case, you had John Adams, the president, a Federalist, and Thomas Jefferson, elected as vice-president, a Republican, the second and third presidents respectively. This amendment cleaned up the Electoral College process by making it specific who would be president and who would be vice-president. This replaces much of Article II Section 1. Following that election, you now have running mates. If no one wins a majority, it goes into the House, and this happened the very next election in 1800.

The XIII- XV amendments deal with slavery, the south and the civil war, more precisely, the emancipation thereof. So, slavery and involuntary servitude are made illegal, their children are made citizens of the United States. They are given full rights including that of voting.

It also strips the rights from those citizens engaged in the civil war, including those that supported it by giving aid and comfort, pretty much everyone in the south. It also restricts the States from recouping costs for the loss of their slaves. The south passed what are known as Jim Crow laws to stop the former slaves from voting, making them pay poll taxes. The Twenty-fourth Amendment now restricts this.

The Sixteenth allows the feds to collect income taxes. The Seventeenth replaces Article I Section 3. which gives citizens the right to vote for their senators, which had been chosen by state legislatures. The Nineteenth gives women the right to vote, and the Twenty-sixth extends that to eighteen-year-olds.

Which brings us to the Eighteenth Amendment, dealing with prohibition, which is repealed by the Twenty-first.

The Twentieth changes the term of the president from it beginning in March to starting on January 20th so it shrinks the time between the election and when he takes office. It also changes the date in which Congress shall assemble from December to noon on January 3 changing Article I, Section 4. The Twenty-second Amendment establishes term limits for the president limiting him to two terms, this again follows history where Franklin Roosevelt was elected to four terms and eventually died in office. There is an inherent power of incumbency.

The Twenty-third gives the right for D.C. to participate in the Electoral College as if it were a State, it was never intended to be a State, just a ten-mile square piece of land for housing of the federal government. Our founders were opposed to it ever being a State.

And last, we have the Twenty-fifth which deals with the line of succession of the president when he resigns or dies. The vice-president shall become president. It also gives a way for him to temporarily step down if he should become unfit to serve and allows him a way to come back if the situation should change and allows the vice-president and his chief officers a way to remove him if he becomes unfit to serve.

Article III of our Constitution requires an independent judiciary. I have chosen to insert a brief explanation of our earliest court decisions.

Article III of our Constitution houses the Supreme Court and as it says all inferior courts as Congress may appoint. George Washington appointed the first justices, and he chose John Jay to be the first chief justice of the Supreme Court. He along with Madison and Hamilton had written the Federalist papers.

In the early days of the Republic, they were circuit riders providing judging duties throughout the circuit courts. Unlike today, where you have a majority opinion published, in those days each judge wrote his own opinions. Along with Jay, Washington chose as associate judges John Rutledge who later became chief justice, William Cushing, James Wilson who had been a delegate to the federal convention, John Blair and James Iredell which made up our first Supreme Court. In 1790, Hamilton wrote the court asking for judicial review of laws before their adoption. Writing for the court, Jay said the courts' function was to rule on the constitutionality of cases being tried, thereby asserting the independence of the court.

In 1791 their first case West vs Barnes. The court decided the case procedurally, that they had to file with the clerk of the Supreme Court within ten days, not a lower court. They had first applied to a lower court, so as a result, Congress changed the procedure to allow lower courts to issue writs.

In 1792, Hayburn's case involved a veteran seeking a pension, Jay wrote a letter stating to Washington that the determination was that the legislative and executive branches had to make the decision, not that of the judiciary, thereby citing the separation of powers as defined in our Constitution. By this time, Thomas Johnson had replaced Rutledge on the High Court.

In 1793's Chislom vs Georgia, Georgia owed an extensive debt incurred during the revolution. Georgia, ignoring the case, refusing to even fight the case in court, believing that they had no standing in a 4-1 ruling. With only Irdell voting in the minority, they found against the state. This ruling resulted in the passage of the Eleventh Amendment which restricts a resident of one State from suing another in federal court. This is a very important case because it establishes judicial review. It also shows how to properly deal with a decision that is so objected to, by this time William Patterson had replaced Thomas Johnson.

In 1794 Georgia vs Brailsford, ruled that debts not forfeited by States during the revolution could be recovered by bondholders. This is the only case ever held with a jury trial. These four cases are the only ones heard during the Jay court.

John Jay ran for governor of New York, won and resigned from the Supreme Court. Washington selected Rutledge as his replacement, giving him a recess appointment as the Senate would not meet again until December. Between his appointment and when the Senate would again meet, he gave an impassioned speech in opposition to the Jay Treaty, and he was not confirmed. So, during his tenure, there were only two cases. Here, Washington gives a recess appointment. I have always contended that because federal judges serve for life, they can't be recessed appointed. No court has ever really decided this issue. Rutledge did the favor of resigning after the vote against him.

On June 28, 1795, John Rutledge became the supreme court justice nominated by Washington. In the six months he served, there were only two cases.

In 1795-United States vs Peters held that the United States had no jurisdiction over a foreign privateer. The privateer had captured a ship in international waters and was not within the jurisdiction of the court. In its ruling, the Supreme Court prohibited the district court from proceeding against the privateer stating that the courts had no jurisdiction over crimes committed in international waters.

In 1795- Talbot vs Johnson's court decision held that even if one renounced their citizenship of a State, they were still citizens of the United States even if they became a citizen of another country, in this case France.

Washington's next nominee for chief justice was William Cushing, who declined to be considered, following that he nominated Oliver Ellsworth who received a near-unanimous vote of consent.

In 1796 Hylton vs The United States came up through the lower court dealing with a carriage tax. They ruled that the tax was not a direct tax and upheld the lower court ruling. The question was whether it was a duty or a tax. If it was a duty, it would be covered under the provision of Congress for tariffs and duties.

In 1798 Hollinsworth vs Virginia involves the passage of the Eleventh Amendment. The question was whether the president has a role in deciding amendments. The court in a unanimous decision found that the Eleventh Amendment had been processed legally, so it could stand. None of the earlier amendments had been submitted to the president either, this fact acted as a precedent. They ruled it was unnecessary due to the two-thirds super-majority required for amendments under the Constitution thereby being a veto proof majority anyway.

In 1798- Calder vs Bull dealt with a will's contents in which a new trial had been ordered. "Article I section 10 No state shall pass any bill of attainder, expost facto (Retroactive law) law, or law impairing the obligation of contracts or grant any title of nobility." Samuel Chase argued that a State had no right to interfere with individual rights and "the general principles of law and reason." He then said that "judges should rely on natural law when reaching decisions... Manner of acquiring property and of alienating or transferring, inheriting or transmitting it, is conferred by society."

James Irdell cited "the ideas of natural justice are regulated by no fixed standard; the legislature had passed an act which, in the opinion of the judges, was inconsistent with the abstract of principles of natural justice." William Cushing agreed stating "the case appears to me to be clear of all difficulty taken either way. If the act is a judicial act, it is not touched by the federal Constitution, and if it is a legislative act, it is maintained and justified by the ancient and uniform practice of the state. These acts were legislative judgments; and an exercise of judicial power."

The court held it had "no jurisdiction to determine whether any law of any States legislature contrary to the Constitution is void... No man should be compelled to do what the laws don't require." Furthermore, the courts have no authority to nullify State laws which violate that State's Constitution.

In 1799 New York vs Connecticut- had to do with a jurisdictional land issue in which there was a dispute over which State the land existed in. The court denied a motion to remove the case from the district court.

In 1801 following the election of Thomas Jefferson, but before he held office, President John Adams nominated John Marshall, our longest serving chief justice, serving till his death. He is also one of the most influential. Right out of the gate, he had one of the most important cases which established judicial review.

In 1801 Marbury vs Madison- Marbury was a judge who had been appointed by John Adams after the election of Thomas Jefferson and just prior to him being seated. Time had lapsed so it was believed it was now President Jefferson who could appoint. Madison at this time was a member of Jefferson's cabinet, serving as secretary of state and refused to issue his credentials so he could be seated. Jefferson was opposed to the judicial appointments by Adams as they were Federalist's. Marbury sued to the Supreme Court the Supreme Court found that Madison had acted inappropriately but didn't order the new administration to comply. This was the first case which dealt with judicial review.

The court moved on to settle a number of important cases, creating respect for our federal judiciary. Prior to Lincoln's emancipation proclamation, the country was half free, half slave, unfortunately this was a time bomb waiting for the court. When they ruled on the Dred Scott decision, there was such a public outcry up north anyway in the free states. They ruled that a slave as property couldn't bring a case suing for his freedom just because his owner had brought him into a free State. Within ten years of this ruling, we were engaged in a great civil war. I am in no way implying that this caused it. However, with the election of Lincoln and the fact that he could appoint justices surely weighed heavy. The south feared his election. Fear of Lincoln and his anti-slavery opinions is what caused the south's secession. Our country had survived the hurtles of slavery, they had tried to hold the country together from the beginning, done all they could from the convention hall forward all the way to the 1860s, but it tore the country apart anyway, costing us immense lives, it's just a matter of history. I have often wondered if we had not had the three-fifths clause, the south would have had more representation in the House of Representatives, so how would that have altered history? There were amendments dealing with this during reconstruction, which made the practice unconstitutional and gave the former slaves absolute equality under the law.

Through these court decisions and the text and original understanding of the Constitution, this is where it now stands, for the moment anyway, a monument in paper for all time. I have been brief, in discussing the later amendments here because there's no reason to analyze something as straight forward as they are. When I look up from the many books on the subject, I have sought to sift through I acknowledge that it took our founders all each working together in their common struggle, each from their independent vantage points, and from the different time point they individually got involved, in their fight against tyranny. And it's for this reason that they all still matter today.

Some were self-made men powerful and rich; many gave their fortunes fighting to set up the Republic, some born poor then rich only to be poor again, some inherited vast estates, but all together, worked for the cause of liberty. If not for them, we would have never declared our independence, there would be no 'constitutioncept' that as a part of the British empire upon which we would still belong, under the king's thumb. It has been my goal to look at the founders as good common men and have taken the editorial privilege of glossing over some things in their lives in order to highlight others. I have chosen which fathers too highlight too. So, based on the truth and colorfulness of their lives in some cases, looking for things which would be interesting.

It is hard to disseminate certain founders who may have been involved, yet didn't publicly speak, leaving almost no record.

This was really the criteria I used. I felt if it were not necessary or undermining to the story of our founding, to come to a common cause in an effort to show why they should be taught, because they do matter! Or at the very least they should to every freedom-loving American!

The biggest reason they matter though, is the Constitution itself. Which is why, I'm including a chapter explaining it!

In my opinion this itself is the greatest gift our founders working together gave us, along with those that updated it over the years. These men especially, in convention assembled, accomplished something so convincingly unique for their time, so be careful in your deliberations and ever cautious in your understanding of the times they lived in, as well as those we do. In the study of our founder's accuracy is vital and I have tried my best to keep things correct with so many sources to sort through, though it is nearly certain that some sources just aren't believable, so I have omitted things I felt were wrong.

Sit back and relax, for the moment anyway, in the knowledge I have given you. So much more could be said, we could fill volumes if we went into the men individually, so I'll end here. Hopefully I have given you a bigger window into the events than what you're understanding previously was. I hope you enjoy your liberty in the promise of what they left us. I hope you realize why the founders still very much matter!

In all truthfulness, the founder's matter because of what they accomplished declaring independence, fighting a war for it, and then setting up a government by the people for the people as they said. For the betterment of all of us future generations, and as Reagan said, were never more than one generation away from tyranny and yes, I'm paraphrasing!

Our Constitution is a vitally important document because it encompasses law which cannot be changed easily. Law is there to govern our way of life so if I were to open statute books and read through them it would encompass almost every situation imaginable because we are a country of laws. Those laws begin with the federal Constitution then goes to the States, and finally legislative action. Our federal and state laws govern almost every question. So, understanding our documents becomes highly important, after all, ignorance before the law is no excuse. Our federal Constitution, through the Bill of Rights also gives us certain guarantees against a tyrannical state. Like an old co-worker would always tell me, knowledge is power. With that in mind, we need a knowledgeable electorate to make decisions at the ballot box which affect us all. My previous book on the subject, Textualism and Originalism in our Constitutional Republic is a gift to the American people.

This was meant to be its mate going over the things that surround the documents. It was and is my hope that it helps to achieve a better understanding. Left or right doesn't matter as much as living in a society where we can all live IN LIBERTY in the way we choose to live, think about it! Our founders did. –

That my friend is why our founder's still matter in their words-

www.ingramcontent.com/pod-product-compliance
Lightning Source LLC
LaVergne TN
LVHW010205070526
838199LV00062B/4509